CATHERINE
THE GREAT

WORLD LEADERS PAST & PRESENT

CATHERINE THE GREAT

Leslie McGuire

1986
CHELSEA HOUSE PUBLISHERS
NEW YORK
NEW HAVEN PHILADELPHIA

SENIOR EDITOR: William P. Hansen
ASSOCIATE EDITORS: John Haney
        Richard Mandell
        Marian W. Taylor
EDITORIAL COORDINATOR: Karyn Gullen Browne
EDITORIAL STAFF: Pierre Hauser
        Perry Scott King
        Howard Ratner
        John Selfridge
        Bert Yaeger
ART DIRECTOR: Susan Lusk
LAYOUT: Irene Friedman
ART ASSISTANTS: Noreen Lamb
        Carol McDougall
        Victoria Tomaselli
COVER DESIGN: Morgan Harris
PICTURE RESEARCH: Susan Quist

First Printing

Library of Congress Cataloging in Publication Data

McGuire, Leslie. CATHERINE THE GREAT

(World leaders past & present)
Bibliography: p.
Includes index.
   1. Catherine II, Empress of Russia, 1729–1796—
Juvenile literature. 2. Soviet Union—Kings and rulers
—Biography—Juvenile literature. [1. Catherine II,
Empress of Russia, 1729–1796. 2. Kings, queens,
rulers, etc. 3. Soviet Union—History—Catherine II,
1762–1796] I. Title. II. Series.
DK170.M35   1986   947.063'092'4 [B] [92] 85–19040

ISBN 0–87754–577–4

Chelsea House Publishers
Harold Steinberg, Chairman & Publisher
Susan Lusk, Vice President
A Division of Chelsea House Educational Communications, Inc.

133 Christopher Street, New York, N.Y. 10014

345 Whitney Avenue, New Haven, CT 06510

5014 West Chester Pike, Edgemont, PA 19028

Photos courtesy of AP/Wide World Photos, Art Resource, The Bettmann
Archive, The Metropolitan Museum, UPI/Bettmann Newsphotos

Contents

CHELSEA HOUSE PUBLISHERS

WORLD LEADERS PAST & PRESENT

ADENAUER
ALEXANDER THE GREAT
MARK ANTONY
KING ARTHUR
KEMAL ATATÜRK
CLEMENT ATTLEE
BEGIN
BEN GURION
BISMARCK
LEON BLUM
BOLÍVAR
CESARE BORGIA
BRANDT
BREZHNEV
CAESAR
CALVIN
CASTRO
CATHERINE THE GREAT
CHARLEMAGNE
CHIANG KAI-SHEK
CHOU EN-LAI
CHURCHILL
CLEMENCEAU
CLEOPATRA
CORTEZ
CROMWELL
DANTON
DE GAULLE
DE VALERA
DISRAELI
EISENHOWER
ELEANOR OF AQUITAINE
QUEEN ELIZABETH I
FERDINAND AND ISABELLA

FRANCO
FREDERICK THE GREAT
INDIRA GANDHI
GANDHI
GARIBALDI
GENGHIS KHAN
GLADSTONE
HAMMARSKJÖLD
HENRY VIII
HENRY OF NAVARRE
HINDENBURG
HITLER
HO CHI MINH
KING HUSSEIN
IVAN THE TERRIBLE
ANDREW JACKSON
JEFFERSON
JOAN OF ARC
POPE JOHN XXIII
LYNDON JOHNSON
BENITO JUÁREZ
JFK
KENYATTA
KHOMEINI
KHRUSHCHEV
MARTIN LUTHER KING
KISSINGER
LENIN
LINCOLN
LLOYD GEORGE
LOUIS XIV
LUTHER
JUDAS MACCABEUS

MAO
MARY, QUEEN OF SCOTS
GOLDA MEIR
METTERNICH
MUSSOLINI
NAPOLEON
NASSER
NEHRU
NERO
NICHOLAS II
NIXON
NKRUMAH
PERICLES
PERÓN
QADDAFI
ROBESPIERRE
ELEANOR ROOSEVELT
FDR
THEODORE ROOSEVELT
SADAT
SUN YAT-SEN
STALIN
TAMERLAINE
THATCHER
TITO
TROTSKY
TRUDEAU
TRUMAN
QUEEN VICTORIA
WASHINGTON
CHAIM WEIZMANN
WOODROW WILSON
XERXES

Further titles in preparation

ON LEADERSHIP
Arthur M. Schlesinger, jr.

LEADERSHIP, it may be said, is really what makes the world go round. Love no doubt smooths the passage; but love is a private transaction between consenting adults. Leadership is a public transaction with history. The idea of leadership affirms the capacity of individuals to move, inspire and mobilize masses of people so that they act together in pursuit of an end. Sometimes leadership serves good purposes, sometimes bad; but whether the end is benign or evil, great leaders are those men and women who leave their personal stamp on history.

Now, the very concept of leadership implies the proposition that individuals can make a difference. This proposition has never been universally accepted. From classical times to the present day, eminent thinkers have regarded individuals as no more than the agents and pawns of larger forces, whether the gods and goddesses of the ancient world or, in the modern era, race, class, nation, the dialectic, the will of the people, the spirit of the times, history itself. Against such forces, the individual dwindles into insignificance.

So contends the thesis of historical determinism. Tolstoy's great novel *War and Peace* offers a famous statement of the case. Why, Tolstoy asked, did millions of men in the Napoleonic wars, denying their human feelings and their common sense, move back and forth across Europe slaughtering their fellows? "The war," Tolstoy answered, "was bound to happen simply because it was bound to happen." All prior history predetermined it. As for leaders, they, Tolstoy said, "are but the labels that serve to give a name to an end and, like labels, they have the least possible connection with the event." The greater the leader, "the more conspicuous the inevitability and the predestination of every act he commits." The leader, said Tolstoy, is "the slave of history."

Determinism takes many forms. Marxism is the determinism of class, Nazism the determinism of race. But the idea of men and women as the slaves of history runs athwart the deepest human instincts. Rigid determinism abolishes the idea of human freedom—the assumption of free choice that underlies every move we make, every word we speak, every thought we think. It abolishes the idea of human responsibility, since it is manifestly unfair to reward or punish people for actions that are by definition beyond their control. No one can live consistently by any deterministic creed. The Marxist states prove this themselves by their extreme susceptibility to the cult of leadership.

More than that, history refutes the idea that individuals make no difference. In December 1931 a British politician crossing Park Avenue in New York City between 76th and 77th Streets around ten-thirty at night looked in the wrong direction and was knocked down by an automobile—a moment, he later recalled, of a man aghast, a world aglare: "I do not understand why I was not broken like an eggshell or squashed like a gooseberry." Fourteen months later an American politician, sitting in an open car in Miami, Florida, was fired on by an assassin; the man beside him was hit. Those who believe that individuals make no difference to history might well ponder whether the next two decades would have been the same had Mario Contasini's car killed Winston Churchill in 1931 and Giuseppe Zangara's bullet killed Franklin Roosevelt in 1933. Suppose, in addition, that Adolf Hitler had been killed in the street fighting during the Munich *Putsch* of 1923 and that Lenin had died of typhus during the First World War. What would the 20th century be like now?

For better or for worse, individuals do make a difference. "The notion that a people can run itself and its affairs anonymously," wrote the philosopher William James, "is now well known to be the silliest of absurdities. Mankind does nothing save through initiatives on the part of inventors, great or small, and imitation by the rest of us—these are the sole factors in human progress. Individuals of genius show the way, and set the patterns, which common people then adopt and follow."

Leadership, James suggests, means leadership in thought as well as in action. In the long run, leaders in thought may well make the greater difference to the world. But, as Woodrow Wilson once said, "Those only are leaders of men, in the general eye, who lead in action. . . . It is at their hands that new thought gets its translation into the crude language of deeds." Leaders in thought often invent in solitude and obscurity, leaving to later generations the tasks of imitation. Leaders in action—the leaders portrayed in this series— have to be effective in their own time.

And they cannot be effective by themselves. They must act in response to the rhythms of their age. Their genius must be adapted, in a phrase of William James's, "to the receptivities of the moment." Leaders are useless without followers. "There goes the mob," said the French politician hearing a clamor in the streets. "I am their leader. I must follow them." Great leaders turn the inchoate emotions of the mob to purposes of their own. They seize on the opportunities of their time, the hopes, fears, frustrations, crises, potentialities.

They succeed when events have prepared the way for them, when the community is waiting to be aroused, when they can provide the clarifying and organizing ideas. Leadership ignites the circuit between the individual and the mass and thereby alters history.

It may alter history for better or for worse. Leaders have been responsible for the most extravagant follies and most monstrous crimes that have beset suffering humanity. They have also been vital in such gains as humanity has made in individual freedom, religious and racial tolerance, social justice and respect for human rights.

There is no sure way to tell in advance who is going to lead for good and who for evil. But a glance at the gallery of men and women in *World Leaders—Past and Present* suggests some useful tests.

One test is this: do leaders lead by force or by persuasion? By command or by consent? Through most of history leadership was exercised by the divine right of authority. The duty of followers was to defer and to obey. "Theirs not to reason why,/ Theirs but to do and die." On occasion, as with the so-called "enlightened despots" of the 18th century in Europe, absolutist leadership was animated by humane purposes. More often, absolutism nourished the passion for domination, land, gold and conquest and resulted in tyranny.

The great revolution of modern times has been the revolution of equality. The idea that all people should be equal in their legal condition has undermined the old structures of authority, hierarchy and deference. The revolution of equality has had two contrary effects on the nature of leadership. For equality, as Alexis de Tocqueville pointed out in his great study *Democracy in America*, might mean equality in servitude as well as equality in freedom.

"I know of only two methods of establishing equality in the political world," Tocqueville wrote. "Rights must be given to every citizen, or none at all to anyone . . . save one, who is the master of all." There was no middle ground "between the sovereignty of all and the absolute power of one man." In his astonishing prediction of 20th-century totalitarian dictatorship, Tocqueville explained how the revolution of equality could lead to the "*Führerprinzip*" and more terrible absolutism than the world had ever known.

But when rights are given to every citizen and the sovereignty of all is established, the problem of leadership takes a new form, becomes more exacting than ever before. It is easy to issue commands and enforce them by the rope and the stake, the concentration camp and the *gulag*. It is much harder to use argument and achievement to overcome opposition and win consent. The Founding Fathers of the United States understood the difficulty. They believed that history had given them the opportunity to decide, as

Alexander Hamilton wrote in the first Federalist Paper, whether men are indeed capable of basing government on "reflection and choice, or whether they are forever destined to depend . . . on accident and force."

Government by reflection and choice called for a new style of leadership and a new quality of followership. It required leaders to be responsive to popular concerns, and it required followers to be active and informed participants in the process. Democracy does not eliminate emotion from politics; sometimes it fosters demagoguery; but it is confident that, as the greatest of democratic leaders put it, you cannot fool all of the people all of the time. It measures leadership by results and retires those who overreach or falter or fail.

It is true that in the long run despots are measured by results too. But they can postpone the day of judgment, sometimes indefinitely, and in the meantime they can do infinite harm. It is also true that democracy is no guarantee of virtue and intelligence in government, for the voice of the people is not necessarily the voice of God. But democracy, by assuring the rights of opposition, offers built-in resistance to the evils inherent in absolutism. As the theologian Reinhold Niebuhr summed it up, "Man's capacity for justice makes democracy possible, but man's inclination to injustice makes democracy necessary."

A second test for leadership is the end for which power is sought. When leaders have as their goal the supremacy of a master race or the promotion of totalitarian revolution or the acquisition and exploitation of colonies or the protection of greed and privilege or the preservation of personal power, it is likely that their leadership will do little to advance the cause of humanity. When their goal is the abolition of slavery, the liberation of women, the enlargement of opportunity for the poor and powerless, the extension of equal rights to racial minorities, the defense of the freedoms of expression and opposition, it is likely that their leadership will increase the sum of human liberty and welfare.

Leaders have done great harm to the world. They have also conferred great benefits. You will find both sorts in this series. Even "good" leaders must be regarded with a certain wariness. Leaders are not demigods; they put on their trousers one leg after another just like ordinary mortals. No leader is infallible, and every leader needs to be reminded of this at regular intervals. Irreverence irritates leaders but is their salvation. Unquestioning submission corrupts leaders and demeans followers. Making a cult of a leader is always a mistake. Fortunately hero worship generates its own antidote. "Every hero," said Emerson, "becomes a bore at last."

The signal benefit the great leaders confer is to embolden the rest of us to live according to our own best selves, to be active, insistent, and resolute in affirming our own sense of things. For great leaders attest to the reality of human freedom against the supposed inevitabilities of history. And they attest to the wisdom and power that may lie within the most unlikely of us, which is why Abraham Lincoln remains the supreme example of great leadership. A great leader, said Emerson, exhibits new possibilities to all humanity. "We feed on genius. . . . Great men exist that there may be greater men."

Great leaders, in short, justify themselves by emancipating and empowering their followers. So humanity struggles to master its destiny, remembering with Alexis de Tocqueville: "It is true that around every man a fatal circle is traced beyond which he cannot pass; but within the wide verge of that circle he is powerful and free; as it is with man, so with communities."

—*New York*

1

"Little Mother" Wins the Throne

On the night of June 27, 1762, the Russian imperial family was, as usual, sleeping in separate places. The empress, Catherine II, was alone in "Mon Plaisir," the little pavilion near the summer palace at Peterhof, on the Gulf of Finland. Her husband, *Tsar* (emperor) Peter III, was with his mistress in the palace at Oranienbaum. Catherine and Peter's son, the seven-year-old Grand Duke Paul, was with his tutor at the Winter Palace in St. Petersburg.

An hour before dawn, the shadowy figure of a large man moved across the unguarded terrace of the palace at Peterhof. He quickly slipped down to the stylish brick pavilion and quietly opened the window to the empress's bedroom. The man was wearing a captain's uniform of the Russian army's Preobrazhensky Regiment, and he knew exactly where to go. He was Aleksey Orlov, the brother of Empress Catherine's lover, Grigory Orlov.

"Wake up, Little Mother," he whispered. "The time has come. Passek was arrested."

Empress Catherine II of Russia (1729–1796), who is also known as Catherine the Great, overthrew her husband, Tsar Peter III (1728–1762), and supplanted him as ruler in 1762. Often indifferent to the social discontent that resulted from her domestic policies, Catherine nevertheless considered herself a champion of the Russian people.

Displaying the architectural extravagance typical of Russian Orthodox churches, St. Basil's Cathedral soars above the streets of Moscow. Catherine's German-born husband, Tsar Peter III, who was accustomed to the austerity of Lutheranism, his baptismal faith, considered Russian Orthodoxy excessively opulent. He alienated his subjects when, in 1762, he declared church property a state asset.

The past week had been a momentous one. Peter III had insulted the two institutions that were the pillars of his political power—the army and the church. To the dismay of the former (which had not been paid for months), the tsar was preparing to start a war with Denmark that his general staff believed would be a waste of time, money, and men. To add to both the uncertainty of the situation and the sense of outrage then permeating the army, it was widely rumored that he had sold out the Russian army to the king of Prussia, Russia's longtime enemy. To the despair of the ecclesiastical authorities, Peter had decided to confiscate all of the church's property for the state. A native of Germany and an adherent of Lutheranism, the austere Protestant denomination founded by the 16th-century religious reformer Martin Luther, Peter hated the opulent and ritualistic Russian Orthodox religion.

Making the nation's predicament still worse, the state treasury was empty, the peasants in the provinces were in rebellion, and people had taken to the streets in protest. Everywhere, political passions had been aroused. Captain Passek, a friend of Grigory Orlov, had been arrested for treason by one of Tsar Peter III's spies. His arrest would be followed by torture, and Passek would almost undoubtedly reveal the names of his associates. The time had come for Catherine and her supporters to act.

Catherine quickly dressed in a simple black gown. She and Aleksey then climbed into a waiting carriage. It was not until she was on her way to St. Petersburg—and also on her way to being the sole ruler of Russia—that Catherine noticed she was still wearing her nightcap.

After changing to a carriage pulled by fresh horses, the two resumed their journey. On their way, they planned to secure the support of the military. Their first stop was at the barracks of the Ismailovsky Regiment. Count Kyril Razumovsky, the regimental commander, had been in love with Catherine since she first came to Russia. A little before 8:00 A.M., Catherine steeled herself and stepped out of the carriage to face the mass of soldiers before her. After one look at the erect and slender figure dressed in black, the men shouted, "Hurrah! Long live our Little Mother Catherine!"

A priest was summoned, and as the officers of the regiment knelt before her, kissing the hem of her skirt, the 33-year-old Catherine took the oath. Under the open sky, she was proclaimed Her Majesty the Empress Catherine, sole and absolute sovereign of Russia. The soldiers, who were wild with enthusiasm, swore allegiance to her.

With the Ismailovsky Regiment behind her, Catherine went on to the barracks of the Semeonovsky

The summer palace at Peterhof where, on June 27, 1762, Aleksey Orlov (1737–1808), one of the Russian nobles who favored Catherine, informed the future empress that her husband had begun to move against his enemies and urged her to seize power immediately.

Regiment. The priest led the way, waving his ceremonial cross. When Catherine's procession arrived there, an excited group of soldiers ran to meet the empress and declare their loyalty to her.

Followed by cheering soldiers, Catherine began to make her way toward the Cathedral of Our Lady of Kazan. As the procession approached the cathedral, troops from the Preobrazhensky and Horseguards regiments came up to pay homage to Catherine. The former announced that they had been delayed by regimental officers who knew nothing of

A Russian Cossack cavalryman. Catherine's overthrow of her husband in 1762 owed much to the support of the Cossacks, whose traditional loyalty to Russia's tsars Peter III had forfeited by pursuing a foreign policy that favored Prussia, Russia's historical enemy.

SEF/ART RESOURCE

The men who surround me are devoid of education, but I am indebted to them for the situation I now hold. They are courageous and honest, and I know they will never betray me.
— CATHERINE THE GREAT
upon becoming empress,
June 28, 1762

An 18th-century Russian mountain guard, one of the thousands of soldiers in the massive standing army that Russia had maintained since the days of Peter the Great (1672–1725), who regarded militarization as an important factor in winning for Russia equality of influence with the nations of western Europe.

the morning's events and had imagined that they were facing a mutiny.

Catherine was now in full control of all the military units based in St. Petersburg. And, with every passing minute, the popular support that she could expect to enjoy was also becoming more apparent as hundreds of civilians appeared upon the scene. When the empress arrived at the cathedral, the archbishop of St. Petersburg gave his blessing to Catherine's having become supreme ruler of Russia.

Proceeding to the Winter Palace through the commotion of cheering crowds and the pealing bells of all the city's churches, Catherine demanded to see her son Paul, the tsarevitch. The prince, his hair tousled from sleep, was brought to his mother, who gathered him into her arms and held him up in front of a window. The people below roared their approval. The palace doors were then flung open so that everyone could visit the new leader. For hours Catherine greeted all who came, from nobleman to shopkeeper, and smilingly received their congratulations.

While talking politely with her people, Catherine kept turning aside to whisper orders to the Orlov

brothers. The most important command was to bar all gates and bridges surrounding the capital. The road to Oranienbaum was to be closed and guarded to prevent the tsar from learning too soon about the takeover of the government.

Meanwhile, Catherine composed a manifesto, or declaration, which she ordered to be printed and then distributed among the people. In it she said: "Our Orthodox church is being menaced by the adoption of foreign rites; our military prestige, raised so high by our victorious army, is being degraded by the conclusion of a dishonorable peace. All the

St. Petersburg, the Russian capital at the time of Catherine's coup against her husband. Here the new empress, having proclaimed herself sole sovereign, met with supporters and ordered her troops to cordon off the city to prevent reports of her actions from reaching the tsar at the palace at Oranienbaum.

Unnerved by his wife's bid for power, Tsar Peter III sailed to the naval base at Kronstadt only to discover that the members of the Kronstadt garrison, like thousands of other Russian soldiers, had renounced their allegiance to him.

respected traditions of our fatherland are being trampled underfoot. So we, being conscious that it is the honest desire of all our loyal subjects, and having God and justice on our side, have ascended the throne as Catherine II, autocrat of all the Russias."

That afternoon the tsar, his mistress, and a group of his courtiers left Oranienbaum for Peterhof. When they arrived, they found Catherine's pavilion deserted. Peter was puzzled, but not for long. A messenger soon arrived with the news that Catherine had been proclaimed empress of Russia. The emotionally immature Peter was beside himself. He burst into tears and fainted, was revived, drank a bottle of wine, fired off orders and instantly canceled them. With one breath, he ordered out his Holstein Guard;

with the next, he insisted he had no need for them. Finally, his advisers persuaded Peter to set sail for the Kronstadt naval base, where he might find support from his fleet. But he refused to go without the ladies who had accompanied him from Oranienbaum, and valuable time was lost as food, wine, wardrobes, and women were loaded onto the waiting schooner.

Catherine moved much more quickly and decisively. She sent a message to the Kronstadt military commanders and gained their support. When Peter's ship approached the dock and his arrival was announced, he was greeted with cries of "There is no more emperor!" and "Long live Catherine II!"

Peter was stunned and collapsed on the deck of his yacht. His advisers begged him to sail quickly to the port of Revel, where the bulk of his probably

An engraving of Princess Dashkova (1744–1810), the younger sister of Peter III's mistress, Elizabeth Vorontsova. Immensely loyal to Catherine, the princess, who rode beside Russia's new ruler in a procession celebrating Catherine's ascent to power, was appointed director of the Russian Academy of Arts and Sciences in 1783.

Attesting to the widespread popularity that she enjoyed as empress of Russia, Catherine's image became popular throughout the empire that she ruled, adorning everyday items such as the snuff box shown here. In contrast, her husband had done nothing that might have encouraged similar gestures of popular affection.

still loyal army was assembled for the invasion of Denmark, but he refused. He might have saved his empire by appealing to these troops, but he was exhausted and incapable of making decisions. He wanted only to take a nap. And that is exactly what he did.

Meanwhile, Catherine, dressed in a uniform borrowed from an officer, was riding away from St. Petersburg at the head of a triumphal procession. Beside Catherine rode her friend the Princess Dashkova, who was also dressed in a man's uniform. Suddenly, the new empress noticed that she had forgotten her sword knot. A young junior officer of the guard stepped forward and offered his. His name was Grigory Potemkin—one that Catherine would not forget.

After reviewing the troops, Catherine received the news that the fleet at Kronstadt had refused to aid the emperor. Delighted, she drew up a document for her husband to sign. It said that he willingly gave up the throne and all rights to the empire forever. On June 29 Peter signed the document without protest, and Catherine ordered that he be taken to his summerhouse on the outskirts of St. Petersburg. There, the former emperor was placed under the guard of the Orlov brothers.

Despite the sudden popular acclaim, Catherine knew that her throne would never be secure as long as the rightful tsar was still alive. Peter III was popularly considered a monster at that time, but Catherine was keenly aware that this view of him could change at any moment. She also knew that nothing could be more dangerous to a throne than a legitimate, imprisoned ruler.

Peter had always been unhealthy, and the strain of the preceding days began to take its toll. He became extremely ill. Although it would have suited Catherine and all her friends if the tsar were to die, she immediately sent Peter's private physician to him, and his health improved.

Then, on the night of July 6, 1762, seven days after she had taken power, Catherine received a message from Aleksey Orlov that had been scribbled on a piece of paper. It read: "Little Mother, he is no longer in this world, but no one intended it so. For how could any of us have ventured to raise our hands against our former sovereign? Nevertheless, it happened. He started a quarrel with Prince Bariatinsky at dinner, and, before we could separate them, he was dead. We ourselves cannot remember what we did. But we are all equally guilty and deserve to die. Forgive me or order me to be executed at once. The sun will no longer shine for me if you are angry, and my soul will be lost forever."

Catherine was crushed. Though she had wished for Peter's death, she would not have ordered it—and with good reason. It would forever have been a blot on her reputation. The next day, she issued a manifesto announcing the emperor's death. It stated that the former tsar, Peter III, had died by the will of God from a hemorrhage caused by violent stomach cramps. In truth, he had been strangled.

Although the members of Catherine's court and many foreign observers were convinced that the tsar had been assassinated, the Russian people, delighted with their sparkling new sovereign, refused to believe anything damaging about her. At last, Catherine was secure on her throne.

It is difficult to do justice to the unshaken firmness with which [Catherine] ruled and cared for her Empire. She was ambitious, but she covered Russia with Glory, while her maternal solicitude extended to the humblest individual, and the private interest of each one of her subjects was near to her heart. People seemed to say: "I see her I am happy; she is my protector and my mother."
—COUNTESS GLOVINE
Russian aristocrat, writing during Catherine's reign

2

The Road to Moscow

The character of Catherine the Great was full of contrasts. She could be tyrannical, but she could also be tolerant. She could be extremely wise or wildly reckless. On some occasions, she was generous; on others, ruthless. She was personally sympathetic to the liberal ideals espoused by progressive western European social philosophers at that time, yet in her official capacity as autocratic ruler of the Russian empire she often conducted policy like a cold-blooded, calculating despot. She was highly self-disciplined, yet very sensuous. But in no way did these contradictions ever result in the dilution of her resolve. In fact, they contributed to the kaleidoscopic and complex nature of the love that she felt for Russia. Although the problems that she confronted later on were eventually to extinguish her capacity for tolerance, it cannot be doubted that she began her reign with a strong desire for good and a belief in justice, kindness, and reason.

Catherine differed from most other rulers in that she was to become more famous for her scandalous love affairs than for her statecraft. Her romantic involvements shocked all of Europe, and the name *Catherine* came to stand for reckless lust rather than genius.

At the beginning of her reign, Catherine demonstrated much enthusiasm for the restoration of justice in Russia, which she believed had been lacking during her husband's rule. Although seen by some as maternalistic and by others as tyrannical, Catherine's frequently progressive leadership helped move Russia out of the Dark Ages.

French philosopher and author Jean-Jacques Rousseau (1712–1778), whose progressive ideas Catherine greatly admired but considered too advanced for Russia. Catherine paid much attention to western European cultural trends, showing particular interest in Rousseau and the other 18th-century French thinkers who inspired the intellectual movement known as the Enlightenment.

But Catherine was by no means impetuous when it came to matters of state. In fact, she was the perfect ruler for the Russia of her time. Her thinking reflected the restlessness and yearning for change that were then just surfacing in the minds of the more sophisticated members of Russian society. Relying on a forceful intelligence and an iron will, she started to organize and civilize the mixture of Asian and European peoples that made up the huge Russian population. In time this extraor-

This 19th-century painting of a town in southern Russia's Crimea region captures the Oriental flavor that still characterizes those parts of the country east of European Russia. During her reign, Catherine made great efforts to promote a sense of national unity among the diverse Asiatic and European peoples which comprised Russia's population.

In political affairs, one should be guided either by humanitarian principles, or by interest. . . . Each sovereign must make a clear decision in one direction or the other; hesitation between the two can only result in weak and sterile government.
—CATHERINE THE GREAT

dinary woman would drag her country out of the
Middle Ages and bring it to a stage of development
where it could at least begin to stand comparison
with the other, more developed European cultures
of the period.

Catherine the Great was born Sophia Augusta
Frederica on April 21, 1729. Her birth was a terrible disappointment to her parents, who had strongly
desired a boy. In fact, it is uncertain whether she
was ever baptized; there is no record of her birth or
baptism in the church register of her hometown,
Stettin, Germany. This small city was the capital of
the principality of Anhalt-Zerbst, which was itself
just one of the many independent, German-speaking
states that later came together as the German Con-
federation and were finally absorbed into the newly-
founded German Empire in 1871.

Catherine's father, Prince Christian August of
Anhalt-Zerbst, was one of the many minor princes
who comprised the German nobility in the 18th
century. Christian August was a loyal, albeit somewhat uninspired soldier; he was pious, reliable,
kind, conscientious, and rather dull. Late in life,
he married Johanna Elizabeth, the 16-year-old
daughter of the prince of Holstein-Gottorp—an ambitious young woman whose family was related to
the royal houses of Russia and Sweden. Johanna
was unbearably bored with her life in the tiny court
of Anhalt-Zerbst, and she was even more bored
with motherhood.

Catherine, a high-spirited, intelligent girl, was
tall and slim, with long, shining brown hair and
startling blue eyes. But her early years were not
filled with any great amounts of emotional warmth.
Her mother spoke with her only to point out her
mistakes or to punish her, and her father, while
undoubtedly devoted to Catherine, tended, like many
other men of the taciturn and militaristic class to
which he belonged, not to be demonstrative in his
affections.

The one joyous aspect of Catherine's youth was
the kindness she received from her governess, Babette Cardel, the daughter of well-educated French
immigrants. Catherine later described Babette as

having "a noble soul, a cultured mind, a heart of gold; she was patient, gentle, cheerful, just, consistent—in short the kind of governess every child should have." Babette had Catherine read the great French dramatists Corneille, Racine, and Molière, and the poet La Fontaine. She taught the child to question all things and to trust her own common sense. On occasion, this created a problem for her religion tutor, who was forced to provide answers to questions such as "If God is so good, how can he possibly inflict the Last Judgment on mankind?" and "What is circumcision?"

Catherine had a great deal of surplus energy. She had no interest in dolls, preferring activities that involved running and jumping. Although she was a princess, she was allowed to play with local children. She was a true tomboy, automatically taking the lead in the aggressive games usually played by boys. She even enjoyed the "unfeminine" sport of bird shooting.

In 1739, while visiting her mother's cousin in Kiel, a city in Holstein-Gottorp, Catherine met her

The fortress shown here is the last resting place of Prussia's King Frederick II (1712–1786), also known as Frederick the Great. Catherine's parents were fairly typical members of the Prussian nobility—her father, Christian August, conservative and taciturn, her mother, Johanna Elizabeth, forceful and ambitious.

Empress Elizabeth of Russia (1709–1761), who appointed Duke Peter Ulrich of Holstein-Gottorp grand duke of Russia and heir to the imperial throne, masterminded his marriage to Catherine. Catherine, though unimpressed with Peter, relished the prospect of the power she stood to gain as the wife of a Russian tsar.

second cousin, 11-year-old Peter Ulrich, who was related to a branch of the Swedish royal family and heir-apparent to that country's throne. As the grandson of Tsar Peter I (also known as Peter the Great) the young nobleman had a good chance of eventually being chosen to rule Russia instead. Ten-year-old Catherine thought he was puny, boring, and stupid; he only wanted to play with toy soldiers. But all the mothers were whispering about this possible heir to a throne, hoping that one of their daughters would one day marry him.

Catherine decided she was not attractive enough to win over the little prince. But she began to check her appearance in the mirror more carefully. In her memoirs she wrote: "The extreme ugliness with which I had been endowed was leaving me. For all that I was only a child, the title of queen fell sweetly on my ears. From that time on, the people around me teased me about him, and gradually I began to think of myself as being destined to become his wife."

Then, on December 6, 1741, a palace revolution in Russia ended the reign of two-year-old Ivan VI and his mother, Anna Leopoldovna. Elizabeth, daughter of Peter the Great, came to the throne. She appointed Peter Ulrich of Holstein-Gottorp grand duke—and her heir. Once in Russia Catherine's cousin changed his name to Peter Fyodorovich and embraced the Russian Orthodox faith. Catherine followed his progress with a great deal of interest.

Noted French actor and dramatist Molière (1622–1673). In her attempts to emulate his work, which she admired for its expressive language and natural gaiety, Catherine wrote philosophical comedies that, for the first time in the history of Russian drama, included parts written for peasant characters.

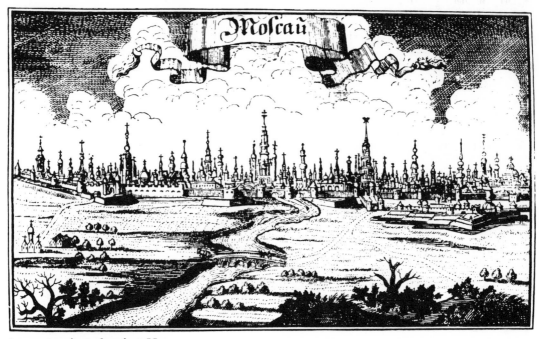

An engraving showing Moscow as it appeared at the time of Catherine and her mother's arrival in the city in 1744. Both women had high expectations: Johanna Elizabeth was eager to embark upon the spying mission entrusted to her by Frederick the Great, while Catherine was determined to impress the Russian court.

In July 1742 King Frederick II of Prussia promoted Catherine's father to field marshal. Two months later Empress Elizabeth sent Catherine's mother a portrait of herself set in diamonds. Perhaps the timing of these two events was just coincidence, or perhaps the empress was making a judicious political move. If Peter was heir to the throne of Russia, he needed to produce heirs of his own in order to ensure the succession. He had to marry. But Elizabeth did not want to make any difficult alliances or dangerous enemies. The choice of a wife needed to be made carefully: She had to be royalty, but she should not be too powerful. A princess from a minor German state would be perfect.

Johanna rushed off to Berlin to have a flattering picture of Catherine painted by the fashionable French artist Antoine Pesne. This portrait was sent to Elizabeth with high hopes that she would select Catherine to become Peter's bride. Catherine thought about the prospect day and night, but love played no part in her thoughts, for she was interested only in the throne.

Then the exciting event occurred. On New Year's Day, 1744, Johanna received a letter from Elizabeth requesting the presence of Catherine and her mother in Russia. Catherine's father was not invited. Two hours later, another messenger came with a letter from King Frederick II. He wrote saying that he would like to see Catherine marry the grand duke of Russia.

But Catherine's father, as a strict Lutheran, was not enthusiastic about his daughter taking a husband who belonged to the Russian Orthodox faith. His daughter was not, thought Christian August, under any circumstances, to change her religion. Catherine's parents bickered for nine days, but Johanna won the argument. On January 10, Catherine and her mother set out for Berlin. They had been invited to visit King Frederick before going to Moscow.

Catherine was on her way to a brilliant future, yet she did not have an appropriate dress to wear. Packed in her trunk were only two or three everyday dresses, a dozen slips, a dozen handkerchiefs, and six pairs of stockings. She had no trousseau at all. But she and her mother knew that Elizabeth would shower them with finery once they reached Russia.

While in Berlin, Catherine's mother had a secret meeting with Frederick, a shrewd and imaginative man. He asked Johanna to be a spy for him at the Russian court; he wanted to get rid of Elizabeth's influential chancellor, Count Aleksey Bestuzhev. Bestuzhev was a sworn enemy of Prussia, and Frederick instructed Johanna to undermine his relationship with Elizabeth.

Johanna was delighted and inspired. She was being sent on "a government mission" of grave consequence. Seized with fiery zeal and now possessing a much-increased sense of self-importance, Johanna treated her daughter more coldly than ever on the journey to Moscow—a trip that took, from the departure from Stettin, almost six uncomfortable weeks by carriage and sled. They arrived in Moscow on February 20, 1744.

In 1743 Frederick the Great of Prussia, always eager to cement alliances that would best further his country's interests, informed Catherine's parents that he considered their daughter's marriage to Grand Duke Peter of Russia politically advantageous.

3

A Royal Betrothal

The court of Empress Elizabeth was religious and worldly at the same time—and so was the empress herself. Elizabeth was extremely pious and spent long periods praying at monasteries; she also loved wild parties and was said to own 15,000 silk dresses and 5,000 pairs of shoes. Though fluent in French, German, and Italian, she was otherwise uneducated. She was also lazy, stubborn, ill-mannered, and sometimes cruel.

Religious practices in Russia—to which Christianity had not come until the 10th century—were very different from those in the rest of Europe. Instead of being in awe of an all-powerful God, the Russians, who followed ancient customs first established by the Greek Orthodox church, turned God into a member of the household. They hung an icon (a small religious painting) in the best room of the house and then surrounded it with family portraits. The Russians also considered brotherly love just as important as the love one felt for God.

Even after the introduction of Christianity, Russian women lived in seclusion. It was not until Peter the Great began to modernize the country and introduced many reforms that women were

The gilded crosses of Moscow's Annunciation Church, built in 1397, which was the scene of royal christenings and weddings for more than five centuries. Catherine, born a Lutheran, prepared to convert to Orthodoxy upon arriving in Moscow, since she could marry Grand Duke Peter only if she renounced her baptismal faith.

Icons, or devotional paintings, such as the one shown here, have adorned the walls of Russian homes and churches for hundreds of years. The exotic and otherworldly art associated with Russian Orthodoxy reflects a mysticism rarely encountered in its Western counterparts—Protestantism and Roman Catholicism.

Peter the Great, the 17th-century tsar whose blending of progressive ideals with a typically Russian autocratic approach to ruling Catherine greatly admired. In encouraging the Russian ruling class to take note of western European cultural trends, Catherine remained very much aware of the similar course pursued by Peter the Great.

Determined to live up to the standards expected of her as Grand Duke Peter's betrothed, Catherine proved to be a diligent student of Russia's language and of its state religion, Russian Orthodoxy. She often studied deep into the night, seemingly impervious to fatigue.

officially encouraged to become more visible in society. Despite Peter's innovations, however, the majority of Russian women still seemed to prefer the cloistered lifestyle that their western European counterparts had forsaken several centuries earlier. It is said that when Peter the Great held parties, he had to send his guards to force the unwilling women to come and join the celebrations. Peter made his second wife, Catherine, empress of Russia, but she chose to pass her days in comparative isolation from the world at large and never learned to read or write. Her illiteracy did not, however, prevent her from taking a measure of interest in affairs of state. When her niece, Anna Leopoldovna, came to the throne, she too remained out of sight.

Moscow, the traditional seat of the Russian court, came as a shock to Catherine. The grand palaces were made of wood. The roofs leaked, cracks in the walls allowed icy air to blow in, and smoky, wood-burning stoves made the atmosphere in her chambers almost unbreathable. The doors were difficult to open and the windows were hard to close. Water ran down the walls whenever it rained, and the sight of rats scampering across the floors was nothing unusual.

The furnishings and china in the city's palaces were not permanent fixtures. Instead, whenever the court left Moscow—as it often did—everything went with it. As a result, the china was chipped, the glasses were mismatched, and much of the expensive French furniture was in a bad state of repair.

At banquets, footmen dressed in gorgeous uniforms stood 10 deep behind the guests. Between each course they first spat on the gold plates, then wiped them clean with a dirty napkin, and finally handed the priceless items back to the diners. The courtiers themselves, who considered such occasions and practices the height of civilized living, were, more often than not, infested with vermin; they spent many evenings picking lice out of each other's hair.

"It is not unusual," Catherine wrote, "to see an immense courtyard full of mud and all kinds of

One of the finest items in Catherine's priceless collection of china, this plate was crafted by British master potter Josiah Wedgwood (1730–1795). Much of the Russian nobility's china was constantly in need of replacement, since the nobles had to bring their household equipment along with them when accompanying the monarch from palace to palace.

filthy garbage, adjoining a ramshackle building of rotten wood, from which a superbly dressed lady covered with jewels drives out in a magnificent carriage drawn by six sorry nags in dirty harness, with unkempt lackeys wearing handsome livery which they dishonor by their clumsy bearing."

Catherine's first few months in Moscow also exposed her to the most disturbing aspect of the social conditions then prevailing in Russia—the

Like the houses in this Russian village, most of Moscow's buildings were constructed of wood and, as a result, were prone to drafts, leaks, fire, and infestation by vermin. The city's palaces were no exception to this rule, as Catherine discovered to her dismay upon arriving in Moscow.

great gulf that separated the nobility and the common people. The wretched and miserable poverty that afflicted the latter greatly dismayed her.

The conditions of life at court in Moscow were much different from those in St. Petersburg, the magnificent city on the Gulf of Finland that Peter the Great had founded in 1703 and made the capital of Russia in 1712. In 1744 parts of the new capital were still uncompleted, and the empress

A 19th-century engraving depicting peasant life in 18th-century Russia. Many modern historians believe that the nature, beliefs, characteristics, and conditions of the Russian peasantry barely changed between the 16th and early 20th centuries. This situation created problems for the left-wing revolutionaries who overthrew the tsarist order in 1917 and began to modernize the country.

chose to spend one out of every three years in Moscow, Russia's old capital. Most of Catherine's life would be spent in the glittering palaces at St. Petersburg and not in the dark halls of Moscow's old buildings.

Judged by the standards of western Europe, the empress and her court were barely civilized, but their somewhat disheveled splendor still impressed Catherine, who was just 15 years old at the time. She tried to gain the affection of everyone, including her future husband, the Grand Duke Peter. To please him, she played with toy soldiers and listened attentively to his incessant and trivial conversation. Faced with Peter's obvious stupidity and his liking for childish games, Catherine humored him by pretending to be equally unintelligent.

Catherine did not, however, make any attempt to imitate her fiancé's hatred for Russia and everything Russian. Whereas Peter longed to return home to Holstein-Gottorp, Catherine made every effort to adapt to life in her new homeland. She threw herself into the study of the Russian language and began to receive religious instruction from a German-speaking Russian priest named Simon Todorsky. He prepared her for baptism in the Russian Orthodox faith.

Catherine's father was horrified by his daughter's intention to renounce for political ends the religion into which she had been born. He wrote his daughter long letters begging her not to abandon Lutheranism. But Catherine, who knew that the marriage could only take place if she converted to Orthodoxy, remained unmoved by Christian August's pleas. She continued to study and to make the necessary favorable impression upon Empress Elizabeth.

Meanwhile, Catherine's mother was becoming increasingly unhappy about the fact that her daughter, as the fiancée of the heir to the Russian throne, now enjoyed greater social prominence than she did. Unknown to Johanna, however, all of her correspondence was being opened and read, so her dissatisfaction was known to the empress. In fact, Johanna's attitude endeared her to nobody. It also

At court there was no conversation, they all hated each other cordially, backbiting passed for wit, and to make the slightest reference to affairs of state was considered high treason. It would have been safe to wager that half the company did not know how to read, and I am not entirely sure that a third of them knew how to write.
—CATHERINE THE GREAT describing the court of her predecessor on the Russian throne, Empress Elizabeth

Disfigured by disease and far from fluent in Russian, the young Grand Duke Peter resented Catherine's charm and her seemingly effortless assimilation of Russian culture. Empress Elizabeth, though alarmed by Peter and Catherine's obvious incompatibility, ignored her advisers' suggestions that their marriage be delayed.

jeopardized the future that Catherine was determined to achieve despite the many disadvantages that still beset her, not the least of which was the nature of her future husband.

The grand duke did his best to befriend his bride-to-be, but his childishness did not, in Catherine's eyes, make his company particularly exciting or desirable. Catherine received another unwelcome surprise when she discovered that the idea of becoming tsar actually terrified the young man. Shortly after Catherine's arrival in Moscow he had confessed to her that his obligation to marry and beget children made him miserable.

But the prospect of ruling that so dismayed Peter fascinated Catherine. She adored Russia and paid much attention to the imperial style that Empress Elizabeth exhibited in her dealings with courtiers and commoners alike. Catherine's eagerness to fol-

low Elizabeth's example can also be explained by the fact that the empress thought highly of her. Once, while Elizabeth was on one of her habitual religious retreats at a convent outside Moscow, Catherine became ill. The empress returned to the palace as soon as she heard the news. For three weeks Catherine was unconscious most of the time, and everyone assumed that she would die. She was bled sixteen times in four weeks—a somewhat medieval method of treatment that was still widely used by Russian doctors at that time, and one to which she would probably not have been subjected in Anhalt-Zerbst. Finally, believing that Catherine was about to die, Johanna suggested that a Lutheran minister be called, but Catherine answered, "No, call Simon Todorsky instead. I will gladly speak to him."

So determined was Catherine to be accepted by

The New Maiden Convent in Moscow, originally a fortress built to defend the southwestern approaches to the city. It was at convents such as this one that Empress Elizabeth frequently conducted retreats, seeking a measure of relief from the burdens of state.

Russia's rulers spent much money on clothing fashioned from expensive fabric such as the silver, gold, and silk brocade shown here. An idea of the importance attached by the ruling elite to owning fine apparel can be gauged from the fact that Empress Elizabeth owned 15,000 dresses and 5,000 pairs of shoes.

Russian society that, in spite of her illness, she had the presence of mind to ask for a Russian Orthodox priest to administer the last rites to her. Word of her request spread quickly through the court, and she won the trust and sympathy of her future compatriots. Gradually she recovered.

However, Catherine's brush with death did little to dispel Johanna's jealousy of her daughter's increasing influence. Soon after the crisis was over, Johanna asked for the length of blue-and-silver-brocade fabric that Catherine's uncle had given her when she left home. It was the only pretty thing that Catherine owned, and she was miserable about having to give it up. Too weak from exhaustion and pain to protest, she handed over the much-prized material. Her ladies-in-waiting were furious with Johanna and told the empress what had happened.

To compensate for Johanna's spitefulness, the doting Elizabeth sent Catherine several bolts of beautiful material, including a new length of blue brocade streaked with silver, and a necklace and earrings worth 20,000 rubles. (It is estimated that in Catherine's time the ruble, the standard Russian currency, was worth about $15 in today's American dollars, which means that the necklace and earrings were worth the equivalent of $300,000.) Grand Duke Peter sent her a fabulously expensive watch that was inlaid with rubies. The generosity shown to Catherine suggests that she was now securely established in a favorable position at the Russian court.

On June 28, 1744, Catherine was baptized in the Russian Orthodox faith. The empress gave her a red silk dress beautifully embroidered with silver, and personally led her into the church. In a firm, clear voice, Catherine recited her confession of faith in perfect Russian, thus gaining still further the admiration of the empress, of her future husband, and of the Russian people. She was baptized Catherine Alekseyevna.

The next day, with much pomp and ceremony, the whole court went in procession to the cathedral. There, the archbishop of Novgorod formally betrothed Catherine Alekseyevna to Grand Duke Peter Fyodorovich. The ceremony lasted four hours, and Catherine's legs became numb. She swayed with exhaustion as they exchanged rings. "The one he gave me was worth 12,000 rubles," she wrote in her memoirs. "The one he received from me, 14,000." At the same time, Catherine was given the rank of grand duchess and the title of Imperial Highness. A few days later, Elizabeth gave Catherine 30,000 rubles for pocket money.

Despite her mother's intrigues and insults, Catherine's position at the Russian court was now vir-

The Cathedral of St. Sophia, in Novgorod. The bishop of Novgorod officiated at the betrothal of Catherine and Grand Duke Peter on June 29, 1744, the day after Catherine's baptism into the Russian Orthodox faith.

tually unassailable. And yet she never ceased to work hard at improving her position still further. She studied Russian more diligently than ever and continued to be sweet and flattering to Peter, whose behavior still left much to be desired. But in spite of Catherine's attentions, Peter flirted with every woman at court except his future bride. Although Catherine often cried about this state of affairs when she was alone, she managed to act as if nothing was the matter whenever she appeared in public.

At about the same time, Catherine's popularity was beginning to displease the only woman who was really in a position to harm her if she so wished—the empress. Elizabeth had never wanted to share the limelight. Vain and imperious, she wanted to be not only the most powerful woman in all of Russia but also to be considered the most beautiful. If any lady at court made the mistake of looking too attractive, Elizabeth was likely to hack off some of her curls, or simply banish her. As Catherine grew more charming and lovely, Elizabeth's jealousy began to eat away at their relationship. Fortunately for Catherine, the empress's animosity did not last.

Shortly after the betrothal, Catherine's relationship with her fiancé took yet another turn for the worse when Peter contracted smallpox. After six weeks he recovered from the disease, and when Catherine was allowed to visit him for the first time, she was horrified. Peter had never been particularly good looking, and his face was now grotesquely swollen and pock-marked. Although he had hoped that his appearance would not seem utterly repellent to his playmate, he realized immediately that she was disgusted. Catherine's reaction destroyed the whole facade that she had built up so painstakingly during the past months. Her future husband now felt that his friend had become his enemy. He withdrew into the company of his toys more than ever before. The probable nature of their impending marriage was becoming chillingly clear: Peter would remain a bitter, paranoid child and Catherine a willful, lonely woman.

I do not like Moscow at all. Such a rabble of priests, so many monasteries, worshippers, beggars, thieves, useless servants in the houses—and what houses, how dirty they are, with their immense grounds and their courtyards that are nothing but muckholes! There is a collection of riffraff of every kind, who are always ready to oppose law and order.
— CATHERINE THE GREAT

Playing with toy soldiers, such as the German-manufactured miniature bandsmen shown here, continued as one of Grand Duke Peter's recreational hobbies following his marriage to Catherine in 1745. Catherine's resentment of her husband's immaturity was aggravated by his decision to give his dogs the run of the royal bedchamber.

Peter the Third,
Emperor of Ruſsia. &c.

4

Marriage and Motherhood

After the betrothal, Elizabeth had been in a great hurry for Catherine and Peter to marry: She wanted heirs. Her court physicians, however, begged the empress to delay the marriage. Their examinations of Peter had revealed that he was still physically immature and unable to father children. Elizabeth resigned herself to this blow to her hopes and glumly agreed to wait for a while.

In the meantime, Catherine learned more about the court (now moved to St. Petersburg), made as many friends as she could, and managed to remain unconcerned about the jealousy which had now become something of a habit with Johanna. She also discovered a new pastime—reading serious books. The count of Gyllenborg, a Swedish diplomat who had known and admired her when she was a child, reproached her for spending her time in ways that he personally thought foolish. "You think of nothing but clothes," he said. "Return to the natural inclination of your mind." He gave her

When court physicians pronounced Grand Duke Peter physically immature and incapable of fathering children, Empress Elizabeth, anxious to ensure continuity of succession, at first agreed to defer the marriage, but later ignored the physicians' diagnosis. Catherine and Peter were married on August 21, 1745.

MARCVS · TVLL · CIC · FLOR · OLYM:174 ·
Orn nider Marci Ciceronis fisha seu sla
Verior in libris exusi imago mei

Roman orator and philosopher Marcus Tullius Cicero (106–43 B.C.), whose biography Catherine read at the suggestion of Count Gyllenborg, the Swedish envoy to the Russian court. Gyllenborg, impressed with the grand duchess's intelligence, constantly encouraged Catherine to improve her education.

the works of the ancient Greek historian Plutarch, a biography of the Roman orator Cicero, and *Considerations on the Causes of the Greatness of the Romans and Their Decline*, a book by the French political philosopher Montesquieu, whose progressive ideas about government were the talk of educated Europe at that time.

Catherine was so inspired by these masterpieces that she decided to write a philosophical essay of her own. It was called "Portrait of a Philosopher of Fifteen." The count was delighted with her essay, which he returned to her with 12 pages of compliments and recommendations.

In contrast to Catherine, who was doing everything she could to surround herself with intelligent people and to improve her intellectual capacity, her prospective husband now seemed happy only when he was in the boorish company of his valets. One, a former soldier, told him that a wife should always be silent and should tremble at the sound of her husband's voice. Another suggested the use of a big stick to keep his wife obedient.

"Discreet as a cannonball," as Catherine put it, the grand duke repeated his valets' opinions to her. The growing dislike between the two of them persuaded Empress Elizabeth that the marriage should take place before the situation became any worse. Against the advice of the doctors, she began to make arrangements for the wedding.

Suddenly confronted with a definite date for the marriage, Catherine grew frightened. She desperately tried to find out exactly what went on in the marriage bed. Her equally ignorant young ladies-in-waiting could do no more than offer theories of their own in reply to Catherine's questions. Catherine, who was not even sure what the difference was between men and women, became so confused that she finally asked her mother. But Johanna was shocked to hear such matters even mentioned. She scolded Catherine for her unlady-like curiosity.

Grand Duke Peter, who was nervous and curious too, met with as little success as his fiancée in his efforts to improve his knowledge of the subject. His valets, instead of reassuring him, terrified the un-

French philosopher Charles-Louis de Secondat de Montesquieu (1689–1755), whose progressive ideas Catherine first encountered under Gyllenborg's tutelage. Catherine's massive legal treatise, the *Nakaz*, or *Instruction*, contained many elements derived from Montesquieu's philosophy, yet defended the necessity of autocracy and serfdom in Russia.

derdeveloped young man with their crude responses.

While Peter and Catherine suffered agonies of uncertainty, preparations were under way for the grandest wedding celebration that Russia had ever seen. The party was to last for 10 days. To provide food for the guests, herds of cattle were brought to St. Petersburg, along with boatloads of fruit, carriages filled with different wines, and carts piled high with chickens—the list of supplies was endless.

In the midst of all this feverish activity, Catherine had, somewhat unsuccessfully, been trying to get used to the fact that her beloved father would not be attending the ceremony. Christian August had been writing letters to Johanna for months, begging her to persuade the empress to invite him to his only daughter's wedding. Elizabeth refused, however, on the grounds that her people would not take kindly to the presence of a high-ranking Prussian at a ceremony so important to the Russian nation. As a result, Christian August was to miss what he thought was the most important day in his daughter's life.

Three days before the event, heralds went through the streets of St. Petersburg to announce the wedding and to invite the people to a public celebration. Then, on the day of the wedding, August 21, 1745, tables piled with food were set out and fountains in the city's main square were primed to spurt wine instead of water.

The wedding procession from the Winter Palace to the Cathedral of Our Lady of Kazan contained 125 gorgeously decorated carriages. The most splendid, of course, was the imperial coach, drawn by eight white horses and carrying the empress and the bridal pair. Catherine's magnificent wedding gown, made of spun silver and supported by a wooden frame from which hung a nine-foot train, weighed as much as a suit of armor. On her head rested a jeweled crown. All through the procession, the seemingly endless ceremony, the banquet, and the ball, Catherine's head and neck ached from the weight she was carrying.

"It was the gayest marriage that has perhaps ever been celebrated in Europe," Johanna wrote to

> *As my wedding day came nearer, I became more and more melancholy. My heart predicted but little happiness; ambition alone sustained me. In my inmost soul there was a something which never allowed me to doubt for a single moment that sooner or later I should become the sovereign Empress of Russia in my own right.*
>
> —CATHERINE THE GREAT
> in her memoirs

51

her husband. That was probably true for most of the guests, but Catherine and Peter were anything but happy.

Catherine wrote in her memoirs that, when the celebration finally ended, "the empress escorted the grand duke and me to our apartment, the ladies undressed me and conducted me to bed between 9:00 P.M. and 10:00 P.M. I begged the princess of Hesse to stay with me a little while, but she would not consent. I remained alone for more than two hours not knowing what I ought to do. Should I get up again? Should I remain in bed? At last my

The building housing the Territorial Department in Moscow, which Catherine selected to house the University of Moscow shortly after her accession to power. The empress took a keen interest in education throughout her reign.

Currently valued at $52 million, the magnificent crown that Catherine wore on the day of her marriage to Grand Duke Peter contains 1,520 diamonds and is surmounted by a jeweled cross.

I came to a terrible conclusion about him within the first days of my marriage. I said to myself, "If you love this man, you will be the most miserable creature on this earth."
—CATHERINE THE GREAT
describing her feelings
for her husband,
Grand Duke Peter

new lady-in-waiting, Frau Kruse, came to me and reported with great merriment that the grand duke was waiting for his supper which was about to be carried up to him. After his imperial highness had made a good meal, he came to bed, and when he had lain down, he began to talk about how it would amuse his valets to see us in bed together. He then fell asleep and slept very comfortably until the following morning. . . . And things remained in this state without the slightest change during the following nine years."

Catherine was not exaggerating when she wrote this. The nights that followed the wedding were as dismal for her as the wedding night itself had been. Her childish young husband played with wooden soldiers in bed, and Catherine had no choice but to play with them too. Because Elizabeth's spies were watching them, Peter and Catherine had to devise ways to hide these playthings during the day; they knew the empress would be furious if she ever found out that at night they were behaving like children rather than adults.

Despite the fact that the need for this charade stemmed from the grand duke's very real shortcomings, it should be borne in mind that Peter was not as simple as he pretended to be. Even while he and Catherine played their nocturnal games, he told his young wife how beautiful he considered many other ladies of the court to be. Peter even told her how much he loved some of them. Catherine was hurt and humiliated.

As time went on, Elizabeth came to think that they had failed to produce an heir simply because they did not see enough of each other. As a result, every time Catherine made a friend, the empress sent the person away. Catherine was also forbidden to write letters, and she was assigned a companion—a "person of distinction," as Elizabeth put it, to oversee her activities and set a good example. The real function of the "person of distinction," however, was to spy on Catherine and to prevent her from flirting.

Much to Elizabeth's aggravation, none of these measures affected the young couple's childlessness.

As month followed month, the empress's spies had nothing to report. In fact, far from showing signs of pregnancy, Catherine began to show signs of physical illness and mental depression. The court doctors were baffled by her condition and gave her all sorts of odd powders and medicines, failing to understand that all she really needed was exercise and mental stimulation from others.

For nine years, Catherine compensated for her loneliness by reading everything she could lay her hands on: histories, reference books, and works of philosophy. By the time she reached age 23, Catherine had greatly improved her level of education. She had not, however, produced an heir. When, in 1752, a young nobleman named Sergei Saltykov arrived in St. Petersburg to take up a court appointment, Catherine finally gained her first real experience of love. Due to the fact that Saltykov was neither discreet nor truly devoted to Catherine, the affair did not last very long. It did, however, set the empress thinking about the unhappy nature of her daughter-in-law's situation. All that Elizabeth wanted was for Catherine to become pregnant. Since it was obvious that the grand duke could not be of assistance, Elizabeth began to ponder the alternatives. She realized that she could easily arrange to have Catherine made pregnant by someone other than Peter. Elizabeth was not excessively concerned about the fact that the child of such a liaison would not be a true descendant of Peter the Great. After all, she thought, neither the grand duke nor the grand duchess was entirely Russian—they were both part-German. The aging empress, now quite frail and increasingly prone to illness, became increasingly preoccupied with ensuring the succession.

Some historians have suggested that Elizabeth's scheming had something do with the fact that Saltykov, banished for his previous indiscretions, suddenly reappeared at court in the spring of 1753. While there is little doubt that he was responsible for Catherine's first two pregnancies (both of which ended in miscarriage), the identity of the father of Paul Petrovich, to whom Catherine gave birth on

This diamond-encrusted imperial crown was worn by Russia's tsars for centuries until 1917, when left-wing revolutionaries overthrew the tsarist regime and declared the country a socialist republic.

I was never beautiful but I pleased. That was my long suit.
—CATHERINE THE GREAT

September 20, 1754, remains the subject of dispute.

Elizabeth, Peter, all the ladies-in-waiting, and several midwives attended the birth, which was both long and difficult. No sooner had the baby been born than Elizabeth snatched him up and, followed by her attendants, carried him to her apartments. Catherine was left alone, lying on a mattress on the floor between two drafty windows; she was tortured by thirst, and exhausted by her labor. The grand duchess was not allowed to see or nurse her baby; the empress attached little importance to her from that moment on. A task had been asked of her—producing an heir—and she had completed it.

After the birth of her son, Catherine became not

only more beautiful, but also hard and distrustful. Following several months of convalescence, she resumed her social life. Catherine's enjoyment of her return to court was marred, however, by the fact that her lover, Saltykov, had been sent to Sweden to announce the royal birth. Catherine was even more crushed when she learned that in Sweden he was flirting with every woman he met.

Early in 1755 a new man entered Catherine's life—Count Stanislaw August Poniatowski. The young Polish nobleman was a friend of Sir Charles Hanbury-Williams, the new British ambassador to the Russian court. Poniatowski was cultured, charming, and romantic—and he fell passionately in love with Catherine.

Reflected in his passion for toy soldiers such as those shown here, Grand Duke Peter's fascination with the military led to serious political complications when he ordered guardsmen from his native duchy of Holstein-Gottorp to join him in Russia. Neither Empress Elizabeth nor her subjects relished the sight of foreign troops on Russian soil.

5

Catherine the Actress

Empress Elizabeth may have taken Catherine's child from her, but there was one thing she could not take: the political strength that Catherine now possessed as the mother of a future tsar. With the power this child gave her, she no longer had to put up with her unbearable husband. In fact, allying herself with Peter was becoming very dangerous; every day he did something new to outrage the Russian people.

On one occasion, for instance, he sent to Prussia for a regiment of the Holstein Guards. He wanted a reminder of his beloved homeland near him. Playing with real soldiers, thought Peter, would be much more amusing than playing with toy ones. But the Prussians in particular were loathed by most Russians, since there had been a long history of hostility between the two countries.

Peter further incensed the Russian people by appearing everywhere in the uniform of his chosen regiment, resplendent in boots and spurs, with a sash around his waist and a huge sword at his side. He thought that this display would add to his manliness, but all it earned him was the hatred of his future subjects.

Admired by the ruling class for her erudition and charm, Catherine also gained the respect of ordinary Russians by practicing careful observance of Orthodox ritual. The fact that Catherine would obviously make an outstanding empress persuaded Elizabeth's adviser Count Aleksey Bestuzhev (1693–1766) to seek to ally himself with the popular grand duchess.

The suave sophistication imparted to the subject in this portrait of Grand Duke Peter bears little relation to his attested characteristics. His boorishness and his tendency to alienate his wife, his subjects, and his advisers greatly contributed to his downfall in 1762.

A 10th-century statuette of the Virgin Mary and the infant Jesus from Constantinople (modern Istanbul), at that time the focal city of Eastern Orthodoxy. The process of Russia's conversion to Orthodox Christianity began in 987, when Grand Prince Vladimir I of Kiev (c. 956–1015) married the sister of Emperor Basil I of Constantinople (958–1025).

His other activities did little to improve his standing in the eyes of ordinary Russians. He only went to church because it was expected of him, and thought nothing of laughing and talking throughout the entire service. He also spent much time in the company of boisterous young women whose reputations were far from unblemished.

In contrast to her dissolute husband, Catherine cultivated an image of piety and virtue. She went to church regularly, and could often be found working quietly in the garden, surrounded by her ladies-in-waiting.

Catherine also continued to further her education. She had absorbed a great deal from the many books she read. From the French political theorists she learned of theories that behind every ruler there was a large public that the enlightened leader would be well advised not to ignore. From Russian history she learned that in Russia, more than anywhere else in the world, the people's love for one particular person could affect the balance of power.

Thus it was that while Peter angered the people every day, Catherine put her knowledge to good use and became increasingly popular. Her behavior was partly play-acting, but it proved her political astuteness. Her religious attitude impressed the traditionally devout people of Russia, and her education gained her the respect of the ruling elite.

The first important person to sit up and take notice of Catherine's political potential was Count Aleksey Bestuzhev, Empress Elizabeth's closest advisor. Since Elizabeth was now old and ailing, Bestuzhev decided to give Catherine his support in order to advance his own career. He helped her prepare for her future position as empress.

Bestuzhev's eagerness to aid Catherine was tempered by his appreciation of the fact that she was a young, passionate, and lonely woman. He realized that she might find another lover any day, and that such a man could upset all his plans by usurping his place as Catherine's confidant and mentor. Accordingly, Bestuzhev decided to find for Catherine a lover who would listen to his advice.

Sir Charles Hanbury-Williams, the British ambassador, had the same thought. The treaty of alliance concluded between Britain and Russia in 1742 was about to expire; the British government desperately wanted Russia to renew it, but so far no one had been able to persuade Empress Elizabeth to negotiate. Sir Charles decided not only that Catherine could help him secure a renewal, but also that introducing her to the right man might be the best way in which to engage her interest. Both Hanbury-Williams and Bestuzhev saw at once that Count Poniatowski was desperately in love with her and that Catherine found him attractive.

Although Poniatowski was not as handsome as Sergei Saltykov, his feelings for Catherine were more sincere and less opportunistic. He described "her black hair, her dazzling white skin, her long dark lashes, her Grecian nose, her mouth which seemed to ask for kisses, her perfect arms and hands, her dignified and noble bearing. . . ." There was no end to his compliments, and he turned out to be just the tonic that Catherine needed.

Catherine thus found herself with two powerful friends and a devoted lover for whose help she would be grateful in the coming months, since, with Elizabeth becoming more ill every day, the political situation was to grow increasingly uncertain. The empress now paid less and less attention to affairs of state. In fact, most of her time was spent applying Oriental and French cosmetics and potions that she hoped would restore her lost beauty. She often drank until she passed out, and her servants, unable to undress her, sometimes had to cut her silk gowns off her body in order to get her ready for bed.

In December 1757 Catherine gave birth to a little girl, who was promptly whisked off to the empress's apartments; this time, however, Catherine did not mind. Remembering the unpleasant circumstances in which she had found herself following Paul Petrovich's birth, Catherine made sure that she convalesced in style. Her husband made remarks about the baby's parentage but stopped when Catherine challenged him to deny that he was the father. Peter, who was in love with his new mistress,

> *For the sake of my Empire, I have robbed Montesquieu, without mentioning him by name. If he sees me at my work from the next world, I hope he will pardon me this plagiarism, for the good of twenty million men.*
> —CATHERINE THE GREAT
> referring to the 18th-century legal and political philosopher whose work profoundly influenced her treatise on the Russian legal code

61

Elizabeth Vorontsova, the niece of Vice-Chancellor Michael Vorontsov, was basically unconcerned. He seemed attracted to the coarse and ugly Vorontsova because, unlike his beautiful, cultured wife, she presented no challenge to him and did not make him feel unattractive.

Peter and Catherine's relationship was going from bad to worse, and their situation was not helped by the fact that Empress Elizabeth's health continued to deteriorate. Throughout the court people were hatching plots over the succession as the empress grew weaker; although Peter was officially next in line for the throne, everyone had a different plan. Elizabeth's advisors, the Shuvalovs, plotted to overthrow Peter and place Ivan VI on the throne. Ivan, son of the deposed Anna Leopoldovna, had been living in a dungeon for the last 17 years. Though deficient in intelligence, he still had rights of succession; he was the grand-nephew of Peter the Great. Vice-Chancellor Vorontsov, however, considered Peter the rightful heir. He also wanted Catherine divorced, banished, and replaced by his niece. Vorontsov, who knew that his position would be much stronger if his niece were empress, did everything in his power to make trouble for Catherine.

Count Nikita Panin, Paul Petrovich's tutor and an old favorite of Empress Elizabeth, was also scheming. He wanted Paul to be declared emperor and Catherine to act as regent until Paul came of age. Other plots involved Catherine, who had her own supporters.

One of the conspiracies to bring Catherine into disfavor with Elizabeth came close to succeeding. However, Catherine managed to suppress the attempt. Bestuzhev and Poniatowski were banished for their parts in the the plot, but Catherine did not seem to mind, for she had found a new lover. He was Grigory Orlov, a lieutenant in the palace guards. He would turn out to be Catherine's most important ally.

The most handsome of the five popular Orlov brothers, Grigory was athletic, romantic, but not particularly intelligent. He was also brave, strong, and greatly loved by his companions in the guards

Her temperament was mercurial. One moment she would be reveling in the wildest and most childish of games; a little later she would be seated at her desk, coping with the most complicated affairs of finance and politics.

—COUNT STANISLAW PONIATOWSKI
a Polish nobleman who became Catherine's lover in 1755 and whom she appointed king of Poland in 1764

Polish nobleman Stanislaw Augustus Poniatowski (1732–1798), later Poland's King Stanislaw II Augustus, whom Catherine first met in 1755. British diplomat Sir Charles Hanbury-Williams, who introduced Catherine and Poniatowski to each other, used their subsequent love affair to gain Catherine's support for renewal of a Russo-British treaty of alliance.

—a unit whose loyalty would be extremely useful to anyone staging a palace revolution.

Following the death of Empress Elizabeth on December 25, 1761, Peter no longer felt obliged to make any attempt to disguise the hatred he felt toward his wife. Catherine was powerless to counter her husband's public insults and threats, since she was pregnant with Grigory Orlov's child. Knowing that Peter could use this evidence of infidelity against her and divorce her, she wore loose, heavy, mourning clothes with long veils.

Empress Elizabeth's body was laid out in state in the reception hall of the palace, and Peter was proclaimed the new tsar. The palace was opened to the public so that they could come and view the body. For 10 days Catherine knelt in prayer beside Elizabeth's bier while the Russian people filed past. As they paid their last respects to the old empress, they were able to see how pious the new empress was. Catherine knew her people were watching. However, while Catherine was acting like a model ruler, Peter was laughing and telling jokes in front of the funeral bier, holding riotous drinking parties and proudly wearing the uniform of the hated Prussian army.

Peter, as emperor, was head of the army and the church. But he chose to forget that the security of his position to a great extent depended upon the support he received from these institutions. He

The Winter Palace in St. Petersburg, where Tsar Peter III moved his court in March 1762, shortly after Empress Elizabeth's death. Peter's mistreatment of Catherine became particularly pronounced following his accession, and served to stiffen the resolve of his disaffected nobles to depose him.

Russian nobleman Grigory Orlov (1734–1783), who was one of Catherine's most ardent lovers and political supporters, played a leading role in the June 1762 coup against Peter III. Orlov's advocacy of improving the condition of Russia's serfs distinguished him from most members of his social class.

made no secret of the fact that he had been a traitor during the war with Prussia which had begun in 1756, sending strategic information to Frederick II at every opportunity. The army was still outraged, and so were many people who had lost sons in the war.

Although Russia had been winning the war with Prussia, Peter suddenly declared a ceasefire, signed a secret peace treaty with Prussia's king on February 25, 1762, and returned all the territory the Russian army had conquered. Then he infuriated his own forces even further by ordering them to wear Prussian uniforms. Next he decided to wage war on Denmark to recover the small principality of Schleswig for his duchy of Holstein. It was an unpopular war, and there was no money in the treasury to pay for it.

Peter then added insult to injury by deciding not only to confiscate all the church's lands but also to change the church's whole appearance. He ordered the priests to adopt the kind of plain dress worn by Lutheran ministers and decreed that all images other than those of Jesus and the Virgin Mary be removed from Russia's places of worship.

The new tsar's policies infuriated both the church and the army—the two pillars of Russian imperial

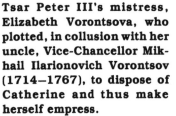

Tsar Peter III's mistress, Elizabeth Vorontsova, who plotted, in collusion with her uncle, Vice-Chancellor Mikhail Ilarionovich Vorontsov (1714–1767), to dispose of Catherine and thus make herself empress.

THE METROPOLITAN MUSEUM OF ART, GIFT OF MRS. T. DURLAND VAN ORDEN, 1962

A grenadier (left) and musketeer (right) of the Holstein Guards, the Prussian regiment with which Peter III had first become associated as duke of Holstein-Gottorp. Peter's 1762 conclusion of a secret peace treaty with Frederick II of Prussia enraged his generals, since the move came when a Russian victory seemed certain.

power. Although, for the moment, there was little that could be done about the situation, the members of these institutions undoubtedly felt that Peter would eventually bring about his own downfall if he failed to moderate his actions.

Peter then began to alienate many of his courtiers by speaking openly about locking Catherine up in a convent or banishing her to Germany. For 17 years he had been humiliated by his wife's greater intelligence, and his patience was almost at an end. Catherine, who was waiting for the birth of the child she was carrying, became anxious, but

Designed by French artist Philippe de La Salle (1723–1805) and executed in silk by master weaver Camille Pernon (1753–1808), this exquisite profile of Catherine attests to the admiration felt for her by the French nobility.

managed nevertheless to show forbearance and humility on the rare occasions when she appeared in public.

In March 1762 Peter moved the court into the new Winter Palace at St. Petersburg. He lived openly with Elizabeth Vorontsova and gave Catherine an apartment at the other end of the building. This arrangement suited Catherine very well; she needed complete privacy so as to be able to give birth in absolute secrecy.

On the night of April 11 Catherine went into labor. To guard against the possibility that Peter might choose to visit her at this critical time, Catherine made good use of the fact that her childish husband considered few things more entertaining than the sight of a burning building. Her faithful servant Chkurin set fire to his own home and sounded the alarm as his mistress prepared to give birth. Predictably, Peter immediately dashed off to watch the conflagration. By the time he and his friends returned, Catherine's baby had been delivered and whisked off to a servant's house. Catherine herself was dressed and ready to receive visitors. Baptized Alexis and given the surname Bobrinsky, the child was raised in Catherine's court once she became empress.

Catherine returned to court 10 days after Alexis's birth, and Peter continued to insult her openly. Meanwhile, Catherine's patient, submissive behavior won her more allies than ever. Finally, in a drunken state one night, Peter proclaimed to his court that he was going to divorce Catherine. When this happened, he said, he would order all the men of the court to divorce their own wives and remarry with women that he would pick out for them. Although he soon forgot about this particularly outrageous plan, Peter continued to treat his wife abominably.

On the night of June 12, 1762, Catherine arrived at an official banquet only to discover that Peter's mistress was present and, moreover, that she was sporting the Order of St. Catherine. In granting Vorontsova this honor, which was officially reserved for members of the royal family, Peter had committed a gross breach of protocol. Catherine pretended not to notice. At the end of the banquet Peter became violent; he embarrassed everyone in attendance by screaming that his wife—the royal Catherine—was "an idiot." He ordered his ministers to throw Catherine into prison, but was dissuaded from this ridiculous course by his uncle, Prince George of Holstein. Catherine realized that on this occasion Peter had probably gone too far.

News of the tsar's scandalous attack on Catherine spread like wildfire. Then, on the night of June 27, Passek's arrest for treason set in motion the events that led to the palace revolution, Peter's death, and Catherine's accession to the throne of Russia.

> *Her features were far from being so delicately and exactly formed as to compose what might pretend to regular beauty, but a fine complexion, and an animated and intelligent eye, a mouth agreeably turned, and a profusion of glossy chestnut hair produce that sort of countenance which a man must have been either prejudiced or insensible to have beheld with indifference.*
> —JOHN, SECOND EARL BUCKINGHAMSHIRE

6

Catherine the Ruler

Catherine threw herself into her job with great enthusiasm. She loved Russia and adored being empress. Every morning she would get up at dawn to begin her 15-hour workday. Right from the outset of her reign, Catherine proved that she could be something of an organizational genius. It soon became apparent that Catherine's concentrated efforts to educate herself had not been in vain. Her intellectual abilities were to be of great value to her country.

As a student of the philosophers of the Enlightenment (a French school of rational thinkers who opposed prejudice, custom, and convention), Catherine had originally been opposed to the system known as serfdom, whereby the serfs (as Russia's peasants were called) were bound by law to the land. Serfs had no rights except those the landowner chose to give them. But when the time came to put her theories into practice, Catherine balked. Far from discouraging this backward practice now that she was in a position to change it, Catherine presented 18,000 serfs to landowners who had helped her come to power, thus treating the common people as objects to be given as gifts. Abolishing serfdom "would not be the way to endear oneself to the landowners," she realized.

French author and philosopher François-Marie Arouet (1694–1778)—known more familiarly as Voltaire—exchanged much correspondence with Catherine, who greatly admired his work. When she heard the news of Voltaire's death, Catherine was moved to declare: "Give me a hundred copies of my teacher's works, that I may put them everywhere."

The heroic and domineering mood of this early 18th-century French portrait of Catherine gives some credence to the legend of how she wore a borrowed military uniform on the day she overthrew her husband.

But Catherine did sincerely want to improve her adopted country. "My only desire, my only wish is for the good of this country in which God has placed me. . . . The glory of the country is my own glory," she wrote. However, Russia's affairs—foreign and domestic—were in appalling disarray after the chaotic reigns of Peter and Elizabeth. Catherine was astonished when she conferred with members of the senate and discovered the true condition of the country.

"The chief portion of the army was abroad, and had not been paid for eight months," she recalled in later years. "The fleet was abandoned, the army in disarray, the forts crumbling. The budget showed a deficit. No one in the imperial domains knew what the revenues of the treasury were. The state budget was not fixed precisely. Almost all branches of commerce were monopolized by private individuals. About 200,000 peasants employed in mining were in open rebellion. In several localities, peasants were refusing to obey, or pay rents to, the landowners. Justice was sold at auction. Cruel tortures and punishments were handed out for small offenses as well as for great crimes, and caused much bitterness. Everywhere the people complained of corruption, of extortion, and of all sorts of injustice."

Catherine realized that she needed to make many reforms, especially in the area of commerce. She approved a decree, originally issued by Peter III, whereby many royal monopolies were abolished. This meant that the public could now participate freely in many different areas of trade that had previously been considered a royal prerogative. In 1762 Catherine permitted the nobles to set up factories on their estates, thus encouraging the expansion of Russia's industrial base.

Catherine worked hard to perpetuate the public's confidence in her abilities. Her interest was not in the gorgeous trappings of royalty but in the backstage workings of government. In fact, paperwork delighted her, and she read every account, report, and memorandum. She attended every meeting of her ministers and the senate, and she sent

A common criminal in 18th-century Russia suffers a form of flogging practiced in that country for hundreds of years, the punishment inflicted with the knout, a braided leather whip.

off letters and orders at a rate that often overwhelmed her secretaries. The empress sometimes became so involved in her work that she forgot to eat.

Catherine had trained her intellect by years of reading such eminent philosophers as Montesquieu and Voltaire. Her lazy ministers were no match for her, and she drove them relentlessly. One day, the members of the Russian senate debated the merits of the administrative system whereby the provinces and towns were under the control of military governors who were not directly accountable to Moscow and St. Petersburg. Catherine asked how many towns there were in the empire, but not one of the senators knew. "Well," she said, "we shall count them on the map." But there was no map of Russia in the state archives. Catherine gave a young official five rubles and sent him to the Academy of Science to buy one. The embarrassed senators had been exposed as unbelievably ignorant.

Catherine's popularity with the Russian public continued to grow. Citizens loved to tell stories about their "Little Mother" 's affection for her people. Guarded by police as she walked to church one day, the tale went, Catherine was suddenly surrounded by a huge and unruly crowd of admirers. As the police raised their whips to strike, the empress spread her arms to protect her "children." Ordinary Russians praised her even more for refusing to hold expensive balls and banquets, as her predecessors had done. In truth, these elaborate entertainments had always bored her.

In the meantime, Count Poniatowski, who was still exiled in Poland, wrote letters begging for permission to return. Catherine did not want him back, however. She loved Grigory Orlov, and furthermore, she had other plans for Poniatowski: She wanted to make him king of Poland. Poor Poniatowski did not want money or power; he only wanted Catherine. But he was obedient. When Frederick Augustus III, elector of Saxony and king of Poland, died in 1763, Poniatowski accepted the crown with a broken heart.

In the midst of all this political intrigue, Cather-

I am perfectly aware that people reproach her with certain little matters with regard to the treatment of her husband. But these are family affairs in which I am not concerned. Besides, it is not a bad thing to have a fault to make amends for. That gives her a motive for spurring herself to great efforts in the pursuit of public admiration.

—VOLTAIRE

French satirist, novelist, and philosopher who figured prominently in the 18th-century intellectual movement known as the Enlightenment

ine was also having trouble with her favorite, Grigory Orlov, who wanted her to work less and play more. Hoping to distract her, Orlov brought to the court a young man who was celebrated for his wit and ability to make people laugh—he was Grigory Potemkin, the officer who had given Catherine his sword knot the day she claimed the throne.

Another important project that Catherine undertook during her first few months as empress was to make plans for her coronation. Peter III had decided against a formal coronation because his idol, Frederick II of Prussia, had himself forsworn such a ceremony. But Catherine knew her position would be strengthened by an elaborate coronation. She ordered a new, solid gold crown and a set of spectacularly jeweled robes for the occasion. In Moscow, the traditional coronation site, preparations

The incorporation of a highly stylized and heroic rendering of Catherine into a map of St. Petersburg bears witness to the city's paramount importance as the seat of imperial power. The city maintained its figurehead status until shortly after the Russian Revolution of 1917, when the country's new, socialist rulers made Moscow the seat of government.

were made to clean up the city for the momentous event. On September 22, 1762, at the age of 33, she was crowned "the most serene and very powerful princess and lady Catherine the Second, empress and autocrat of all the Russias."

Ever since her accession to the throne, Catherine had been eager to obtain the good will of the Russian Orthodox clergy. She canceled the government takeover of church property that Peter had initiated. However, the serfs who had been owned by the church openly rebelled against becoming once more the property of the church's leaders,

The Equality of the Citizens requires Institutions so well adapted as to prevent the Rich from oppressing those who are not so wealthy as themselves.
—CATHERINE THE GREAT
in her *Nakaz*, a treatise intended to guide a commission framing a new Russian legal code

who had been extremely harsh masters. Catherine decided to forestall the possibility of a major uprising by keeping the church lands after all, reasoning that the profits from the land would at least ease her financial problems. The churchmen took a dim view of her decision. The powerful archbishop of Rostov criticized Catherine, daring to call her "one of those who raise their hand against the temples and holy places."

Catherine responded fiercely: "You are the successors to the Apostles who were commanded by God to teach mankind to despise riches, and who

> *Monsieur Diderot, I have listened with greatest pleasure to all the inspirations of your brilliant mind; but all your grand principles, which I understand very well, would do splendidly in books and very badly in practice. You work only on paper, which accepts anything, is smooth and flexible, and offers no obstacles, while I, poor Empress, work on human skin, which is far more sensitive and touchy.*
> —CATHERINE THE GREAT
> writing to Denis Diderot

The Coronation of Catherine II, by Stefano Torelli (1712–1784). In contrast to her husband, who refused to stage such a ceremony on the grounds that his idol, Frederick II of Prussia, had abstained from holding a similar propaganda exercise, Catherine used her coronation to make the greatest possible impression on her subjects.

77

Russian Orthodox clergymen conduct an elaborate ceremony in a cathedral. When Catherine declared the church a state institution and its property a state asset in 1764, the lack of opposition that she encountered convinced her that the clergy would never seriously threaten her supremacy.

were themselves poor men. How can you presume, without offending your own consciences, to own such riches, such vast estates? If you wish to obey the laws of your own order, if you wish to be my most faithful subjects, you will not hesitate to return to the state that which you unjustly possess."

In February 1764 Catherine signed a decree that made the Russian Orthodox church a state institution and its property a state asset. A million serfs were freed by the decree. The hostile archbishop was demoted and exiled to a monastery, and Catherine made a pilgrimage to Rostov, where she set up a silver shrine to Saint Dimitri. The Russian people were more impressed than ever by her piety.

This battle with the church taught Catherine something very important. She had thought that, as a former Protestant and a usurper of the throne, she was indebted to the clergy for her power. Now she realized that she was dealing with men who could be intimidated by a show of royal will. The clergy, she realized, would never make a very dangerous enemy.

At around the same time that Catherine emerged victorious from her struggle with the church, she began to take an increasingly keen interest in befriending distinguished foreigners. She had been corresponding with the French writer Voltaire, who was to become her most effusive western European intellectual admirer, since 1763. She was also in contact with two other prominent French thinkers—Denis Diderot and Jean d'Alembert. She even invited d'Alembert to come to Russia and continue to work on his *Encyclopedia* while acting as a tutor to the young Grand Duke Paul. D'Alembert, recalling the announcement of Peter III's untimely death, politely refused. He confided to Voltaire that he was not eager to visit a country where "people are apt to die so suddenly."

Despite this rebuff, Catherine's desire to earn the respect of these philosophers remained undiminished. She hoped to impress these founders of the intellectual movement known as the Enlightenment with a whole series of liberal projects: a home for orphans, a school for midwives; a public health

French encyclopedist and philosopher Denis Diderot (1713–1784), whose library Catherine purchased when he encountered financial difficulties. The empress then allowed Diderot to keep his books indefinitely, an act of graciousness for which Diderot thanked her in person in 1774.

Empress Catherine walks one of her dogs in a St. Petersburg park. Catherine, who greatly enjoyed the company of her pets, allowed her dogs to breakfast with her.

department; and an institution for educating daughters of the nobility.

Catherine sent yearly pensions to Voltaire and Friedrich Melchior Grimm, a celebrated journalist and critic whose writings helped to spread the liberal ideas of the French intellectuals through the courts of Europe. When Diderot, d'Alembert's co-editor on the *Encyclopedia*, ran out of money and was forced to sell his library, Catherine said that it would be cruel to separate a scholar from his books. She bought his library, allowing him to keep it with him in his home in Switzerland until he died. Her friend Grimm said: "Thirty years of labor have not brought Diderot the smallest recompense. It has pleased the empress of Russia on this occasion to pay the debt of France."

Catherine spent a great deal of money on her philosophers, hoping to improve the world's image of herself and her country. It was a good investment: Instead of calling Russia a backward nation

British physician Dr. Edward Jenner (1749–1823), the pioneer of vaccination, treats a patient in 1796. Catherine's submission to this form of treatment during a smallpox epidemic greatly increased her subjects' acceptance of medical innovations.

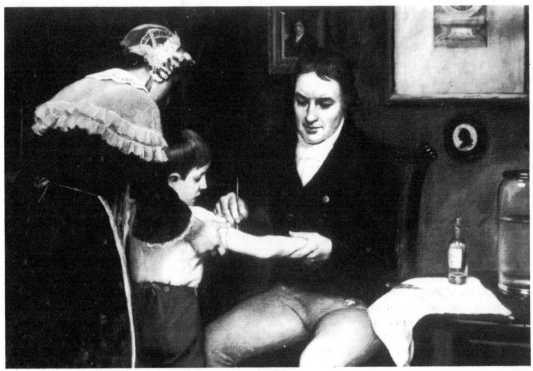

filled with savages and wolves, cultured Europeans began to say that intelligence and humanity were Russia's guiding lights. The empress further enhanced her image by inviting doctors, dentists, architects, engineers, artisans, and craftspeople to Russia from all over the world. On the economic front, she stopped state intervention in commerce, and built many new roads. Catherine's interest in medicine particularly benefited her country when, during a smallpox epidemic, she sent to London for Dr. Thomas Dimsdale, one of the pioneers of smallpox inoculation. At a time when inoculation was a new and unfamiliar form of preventive medicine, Catherine courageously submitted to the treatment. She wanted to set an example for her people and help them to overcome their fear of such innovations.

One of Catherine's greatest achievements was to rewrite Russia's confusing and antiquated code of law. She considered her *Nakaz*, or instructions for the revision of the legal code, the most important work of her life. The document, which was published in 1767, had to be read aloud to the senate, because most of the members of that body could neither read nor write.

When she was not working, Catherine enjoyed a variety of pastimes. She loved dogs, and always kept four or five. Every morning, she shared a bowl of sugar with biscuits and cream with her beloved pets. She drank her coffee strong enough to stun the average person—one pound of the substance to four cups of water. She liked to take the lead in discovering unusual foods. One evening, she dined on a revolutionary new vegetable—the potato. This strange "Indian food" was regarded with suspicion by Russian peasants, who called it "the devil's weed." Catherine, however, decided potatoes were delicious, and urged her minister of agriculture to encourage their cultivation in Russia.

Catherine never allowed the pleasure that she derived from her intellectual and domestic activities to distract her from the harsher realities of politics. She continued to worry about Peter the Great's grand-nephew, Ivan VI, who was still living

This teapot, crafted for Catherine by German master silversmith Johann Heinrich Blohm, is one of the many fine pieces that the empress commissioned from Europe's leading artisans during her reign.

Catherine's son Paul Petrovich (1754–1801), the future Tsar Paul I, became the leading contender for the Russian throne following the death, in 1764, of Peter the Great's grandnephew Ivan VI, whom Empress Elizabeth had ousted in 1741.

in the dungeon to which Empress Elizabeth had sent him in 1741. Ivan had a legitimate claim to the tsar's crown, and Catherine feared that he would one day be rescued by his supporters and present a direct challenge to her rule. Known only as "Prisoner Number 1," Ivan had two full-time guards who had orders from the empress to kill him if he were ever approached by a stranger.

At last, in 1764, a fanatical young army officer, who believed that God had appointed him to restore the skinny, nervous redheaded prisoner to the throne of Russia, made an attempt to rescue the unfortunate Ivan. The prisoner was immediately killed by his guards. Catherine's throne had once again been secured by a murder that she had not personally ordered but to which she did not object. Now the only person left to contest her claim to the throne was her own son, Tsarevitch Paul.

German silversmith Johann Heinrich Blohm also created this gilt and silver coffeepot for Catherine, who made her coffee so strong that many would have found it completely unpalatable.

7

Love and Power

In 1772 Grigory Orlov, who had been spending more and more of his time with other women, was finally dismissed from court. But Catherine was generous, and gave her ex-lover 100,000 rubles outright, an annual pension of 15,000 rubles, furniture, silver, paintings, a marble palace, and 6,000 serfs. Following a brief affair with a dull but handsome young officer named Alexander Vasilchikov, Catherine discovered a more substantial replacement for her once-beloved Orlov in 1774.

Her new lover was the witty, 35-year-old Grigory Potemkin. An enormous man who had lost an eye due to illness, Potemkin was energetic, masculine, and brilliant. He captured Catherine's imagination as no other man ever had.

The empress, now 45 years old, abandoned herself completely to her love of Potemkin. She had a number of names for him—little Grisha, dear plaything, tiger, lion of the jungle, and my dearest doll. She wrote passionate letters to him: "Darling, what comical stories you told me yesterday! I can not stop laughing when I think of them. . . . We spend four hours together without a shadow of boredom, and it is always with reluctance that I leave you. My dearest pigeon, I love you very much. You are

GIRAUDON/ART RESOURCE

This early 19th-century statue was designed to convey an impression of Catherine's prominent place in history. The draped female figure (representing one of the muses—mythical Greek deities that purportedly acted as sources of creative inspiration) holds a plaque showing Catherine wearing a laurel wreath, which symbolizes victory.

Russian soldier and statesman Grigory Potemkin (1739–1791), whom some suspect Catherine secretly married in 1774. In 1783, in recognition of the military and political brilliance that he had displayed in his annexation of the Crimea, Catherine named Potemkin prince of Tauris (the classical Greek name for the region).

handsome, intelligent and amusing. My head is like that of a cat in heat."

Potemkin was a vain, jealous, and temperamental man whose moods varied between cheerfulness and deep depression. Catherine, however, was more than equal to the tiresome aspects of his nature. Once, when Potemkin accused Catherine of having had 15 lovers, the empress blithely retorted that she had known only five. When he accused her of still being in love with a former paramour, Catherine simply laughed. In the depths of his despair, Potemkin would often not dress or eat for days. He and Catherine quarreled all the time, and yet they grew closer as each day passed.

Although there is little evidence to support the fact, some believe that Catherine married Potemkin. There may have been a secret wedding in the little church of St. Samson in St. Petersburg in 1774, but any documents that would prove it have since disappeared. There are, however, 23 letters from Catherine to Potemkin in which she refers to him as "dearest husband," and "my dear spouse."

The empress's love affairs took place against an ever-changing backdrop of political upheaval on both the domestic and foreign fronts. In 1772 Catherine had joined forces with Frederick William II of Prussia and Maria Theresa, empress of Austria, in dividing a large portion of Poland between their three states. The Austrian diplomat Count Wenzel von Kaunitz wrote, "The Russian empress's political program is a masterpiece of statesmanship, admirable in conception and well considered in every detail; it cannot be sufficiently praised." A costly war with Turkey that had begun in 1768 ended in 1774 with a tremendous Russian victory, and yielded Catherine a vastly expanded kingdom and millions of rubles from the defeated Turks. Her importance in the eyes of Europeans grew considerably. In 1773 and 1774 Catherine had been seriously concerned about a peasant rebellion led by Yemelyan Pugachov, an army deserter who claimed to be Tsar Peter III. After much blood— both aristocratic and common—had been shed, Pugachov was captured, tried, and beheaded.

With such a magnificent record as head of state, Catherine should not have had to worry about her son Paul's threat to her claim to the throne. But the tsarevitch loathed his mother, mainly because he believed that she had killed his father, Peter III. It was not until after Catherine's death, when her personal papers were found, that Paul read what Aleksey Orlov had written on the night of Peter's death. "My God," Paul is reported to have said, "my mother was innocent."

Catherine's relationship with her son was made especially difficult by the fact that Paul took after Peter III in character. He even developed an almost worshipful attitude toward Frederick William II of Prussia, just as Peter had. He married a German princess who converted to the Russian Orthodox faith and was renamed Natalia. After Natalia died in childbirth in 1776, Paul married Maria, another

Empress Maria Theresa of Austria (1717–1780) confers with her minister of state, Count Wenzel von Kaunitz (1711-1794). In 1772 Maria Theresa joined with Catherine and Frederick II of Prussia in effecting the partial division of Poland between their respective countries.

German princess. Paul and Maria's first child, Alexander, was born in 1777.

Although Catherine had promised herself that she would never be like Elizabeth, she eventually came to act in much the same way as her predecessor. Even her relationship with Paul had an uncanny similarity to the one that had existed between Elizabeth and Peter. And when Alexander was born, Catherine carried him off to her own apartments—just as, so many years earlier, Elizabeth had taken Paul away from her. Unlike Elizabeth, she did let

Russian Cossack cavalryman and revolutionary Yemelyan Pugachov (1744–1775) was the leader of a peasant rebellion that gave Catherine serious cause for concern from 1773 until 1774, when her armies finally inflicted a crushing defeat on his numerous but poorly disciplined forces.

An 18th-century Turkish cavalryman, one of the thousands of soldiers in the armies of the Ottoman Turkish empire. The centuries-old competition between Russia and Turkey for control of the Black Sea region erupted into a major war in 1768. The victory gained by Catherine's forces in 1774 resulted in a considerable expansion of Russia's territory.

> *Had I been destined as a young woman to get a husband whom I could have loved, I would have never changed toward him. The trouble is that my heart is loath to remain even one hour without love.*
> —CATHERINE THE GREAT
> writing to her lover Grigory
> Potemkin in 1774

Maria and Paul see their child occasionally, but eventually she took complete control of the child's upbringing. She taught him to read, invented games for him to play, lay on the floor with him for hours, and even designed a loose, comfortable garment for him to wear. Catherine encouraged Alexander to believe in the goodness of man. She wrote fables and fairy tales for him. When Paul's second son, Constantine, was born, Catherine took charge of him, too.

Increasingly, throughout her reign, the empress developed an interest in collecting art. She commissioned agents to scour Europe for masterpieces; her purchases included works by Titian, Raphael, Guido Reni, Poussin, Rembrandt, Van Dyck, Veronese, Clouet, Watteau, Murillo, and Teniers. Catherine admitted that she knew little about painting, but that she loved to amass valuable pictures. "It is not love of art," she once confessed, "it is greed. I am a glutton."

After a few years, Catherine's passionate relationship with Potemkin began to cool. However, Potemkin, who enjoyed power and had a genius for strategy, decided not to let his fall from Catherine's favor be his absolute undoing. If he could not be her lover, he thought, he would be her matchmaker—and her eternal friend. Potemkin found successors to his former position of favor. As each one was dismissed by the empress, he was presented with estates, serfs, a lifetime annuity, and other "little gifts."

Catherine's attitude toward all her love affairs was straightforward and uncomplicated. She thought of physical satisfaction as a completely natural need, neither amusing nor shameful. Even in a court as sophisticated as hers, however, her views on sex raised many eyebrows. The cynical French ambassador, referring to the fact that Catherine's lovers were always well rewarded for their services, wrote to his brother, "You must agree that it is not a bad line of work." Others found Catherine's behavior deeply shocking. The British ambassador called Catherine's court a "scene of depravation and immorality."

None of this controversy bothered the empress, who serenely continued to acquire one lover after another. When she was 50, she fell in love with the handsome, 24-year-old Alexander Lanskoy, who had been brought up in the palace with Alexis Bobrinsky, Catherine's son by Grigory Orlov. Lanskoy, who had known Catherine all his life, delighted her with his pleasant disposition and eagerness to study Russian history. She was devastated when he suddenly died of diphtheria in 1784, at the age of 29.

The whole reign of this monarch has been marked by events relating to her love of glory. The many institutions founded by her apparently exist for the good of the nation. In fact they are simply symbols of her love of glory, for if she really had the nation's interest at heart, she would, after founding them, have also paid attention to their progress.

—PRINCE M. M. SHCHERBATOV
Russian nobleman of Catherine's day who strongly criticized her reign in his book *On the Corruption of Morals in Russia*

Catherine's son Paul Petrovich was taken from his mother by Empress Elizabeth shortly after his birth. Similarly, when Paul's son Alexander (1777–1825) was born, Catherine raised the boy herself, in order to groom him as heir to the throne.

In the meantime, Catherine's ex-lover Potemkin had been working busily to annex the Crimea, a peninsula on the Black Sea. Once a powerful enemy of Russia, it was the last piece of the medieval Mongol empire. Potemkin was successful, and Russia gained control of both the Black Sea and the Caspian Sea in 1783. In her gratitude for these great services, Catherine bestowed upon Potemkin the title of prince of Tauris (the classical Greek name for the Crimea) and he began to cultivate the lifestyle of an Oriental potentate.

The Russian nobility's property, including mansions such as this one, was confiscated by the socialist government that took control of the country in 1917. The social inequalities that Russia's new rulers then sought to eliminate had existed for centuries, enshrined in such legislation as Catherine's 1785 Nobles' Charter, which vastly extended the nobles' privileges.

Catherine continued to devote her boundless energy to her country's government and culture. She astonished Europe's intellectuals by appointing a woman—her friend Princess Dashkova—as director of the Russian Academy of Science. In 1780 Catherine had issued the "Armed Neutrality Act," which guaranteed freedom of navigation and trade to countries that were not at war, and, in 1783, she had founded the Russian Academy of Letters. Several scientific expeditions were sent to study the borderlands of Russia, and the Scientific Society was established at the University of Moscow. Catherine herself, to help overcome her grief at Lanskoy's death, began to study the Finnish and Turkish languages, as well as some of the

Princess Dashkova, a loyal ally of Catherine, whom the empress appointed director of the Russian Academy of Arts and Sciences in 1783. Relations between the two women deteriorated when Dashkova authorized publication of a play that Catherine considered tainted with republican sentiment.

foreign dialects spoken within Russia.

In 1785 Catherine passed the Nobles' Charter, which gave the ruling classes even greater privileges than those they had enjoyed under Peter III and released them from the duty of military service. The charter also made the serfs the legal private property of the nobility.

In the eyes of the nobles, serfs were hardly human. A pedigreed dog cost 2,000 rubles, and a peasant girl cost less than 100 rubles. A child could be bought for a few kopecks; a good cook or a musician might run as high as 800 rubles. Although she had been horrified by serfdom when she arrived in Russia as a young woman, Catherine eventually became accustomed to treating peasants like livestock. In fact, during her reign she gave more than 800,000 people to various nobles as gifts and rewards.

In January 1787, in order to show how much he had accomplished, Potemkin invited Catherine and her court to make a grand state visit to the province he governed, the newly acquired Crimea. Joseph II of Austria and his chamberlain, Prince Charles de Ligne, as well as Catherine's favorites among the European diplomats who were stationed in Russia, were also invited.

The empress and the royal party made the journey—which covered thousands of miles and took six months—by sleigh, ship and carriage. They were accompanied by hundreds of servants. Eager to impress Catherine, Potemkin spared no expense in making her Crimean visit one of the most fantastic and lavish ever staged. The party saw only prosperous villages and happy, well-fed peasants—because Potemkin had removed all the beggars and other unattractive people, and had ordered gaily painted false fronts built to hide the dilapidated hovels that lined the way. Potemkin arranged banquets, ballets, concerts, mock battles, naval demonstrations, and whole armies of wildly costumed horsemen to dazzle the company. Catherine enjoyed herself thoroughly.

At the age of 60, Catherine still had a beautiful complexion and sparkling eyes, but she was heavy and shapeless, and most of her teeth were gone. Nevertheless, she still impressed others with her elegance and royal bearing, and she continued to seek the company of young men. In 1789 she took as a lover Plato Alexandrovich Zubov, a 22-year-old lieutenant of the guard. Unlike all her recent lovers, Zubov was not selected by Potemkin, who was far away in the Crimea. Zubov was introduced to Catherine by a group of nobles who hated Potemkin. He was the most handsome of her young men, and she adored him.

The title of the nobility is hereditary and stems from the quality and virtue of leading men of antiquity who distinguished themselves by their service. . . . It is to the advantage of both the Empire and the Crown, as it is also just, that the respectful title of the nobility be maintained and approved firmly and inviolably.

—quoted from the Nobles' Charter, issued by Catherine the Great in 1785

A 19th-century British illustration lampoons Catherine's 1787 tour of the Crimea, where Potemkin, in an effort to impress his sovereign with his efficient governorship of the province, had false fronts put on the peasants' hovels and ordered the removal of beggars and other "undesirables" from the empress's route.

8

The End of Catherine's Reign

Catherine once made a list of her political achievements for her friend Friedrich Grimm: regional governments established, 29; towns built, 144; treaties and agreements concluded, 30; victories won, 78; memorable edicts issued, laws established, or institutions founded, 88; and decrees to benefit the people, 123.

Catherine's achievements were, indeed, considerable, and evidence of the fact that she knew how to command and how to get things done. Austria's Emperor Joseph II was moved to write of Catherine's actions thus: "In Germany and France, we would never have dared to do what has been done [in Russia]. Here human life and effort count for nothing; here one can build roads, ports, fortresses, and palaces on marshland; one can plant forests in the desert; all without paying the workers, who never complain even though they lack for everything, sleep on the ground and often suffer from hunger. The master orders, the slave obeys."

Such was the country that Sweden invaded in 1788, hoping to regain its former territories in Finland. St. Petersburg almost fell, but Catherine's navy stopped the Swedes and peace was restored

An 18th-century cartoon satirizes the first partition of Poland, which took place in 1772. Pointing to a map of the much-disputed country are (left to right): Catherine; Stanislaw II Augustus Poniatowski, whom Catherine created king of Poland in 1764; Emperor Joseph II of Austria (1741–1790); and Frederick II of Prussia.

Emperor Joseph II of Austria criticized Catherinian Russia's expansionist foreign policy and its considerable economic development on the grounds that both were accomplished at the expense of the serfs.

in 1790. Catherine, who was at that time very much involved in her relationship with Zubov, was immensely pleased with this victory. Potemkin, however, found little to like about this situation. Rumors had reached him that Zubov was poisoning Catherine's mind against him. Early in 1791 he raced back to St. Petersburg from the Crimea to see if this arrogant young man was as close to the empress as he had heard. Potemkin was devastated when he discovered that it was true that Zubov had replaced him in Catherine's affections. Five months later, after a long bout with fever, Grigory Potemkin was dead at the age of 52, shattered by the loss of his empress.

When Catherine received the news, she was heartbroken. Potemkin had been her lover, friend, advisor, minister, military leader, and confidant. He was irreplaceable. He had increased the territory of Russia by one-third, populated new lands, built cities in the wilderness, dug ports, planted vineyards, established universities, planned parks, built ships, and won battles. His death was a crushing blow to Catherine, but she hid her misery and concentrated on her work.

In 1793 foreign affairs returned to the top of Catherine's political agenda when rebel Polish troops headed by General Thaddeus Kosciuszko attacked the Russian troops in Warsaw, Poland. Inspired by the French Revolution, which had been in progress since 1789, guerrillas from all over Poland joined him. Catherine, who had been unable to exert any influence on France's internal struggles, was by this time especially furious at the course that events had taken in France. The French revolutionaries had sent their king, Louis XVI, to the guillotine in January 1793, and Catherine's horror at this killing had been made worse by her belief that the liberal ideas of her once-beloved philosophers, Montesquieu, Voltaire, Rousseau, and Diderot had contributed to the revolution and its bloody results. On October 22, 1794, Russian soldiers entered Warsaw's suburb of Praga and killed everyone they could find. Kosciuszko was captured, and Poniatowski, forced to give up his throne, was impris-

Generally speaking, women are more prone to despotism than men; and as far as she is concerned, it can justly be averred that she is in this particular a woman among women.
—PRINCE M. M. SHCHERBATOV

oned on Catherine's orders.

For months, Russia, Austria, and Prussia wrangled over what was left of Poland. But in the end Catherine took the biggest part and increased the number of her subjects once again.

When Catherine came to the throne, the population of Russia had been 20 million. After the annexation of the Crimea, all her military victories, and the taking of Polish lands, Russia's population rose to 36 million. Her country was more powerful and more influential than it had ever been before, and Catherine now felt that she could proudly take her place among history's other great monarchs.

In addition to directing the affairs of the nation, Catherine had been arranging the lives of her own family. In 1793 her 16-year-old grandson Alexander was married to a 15-year-old German princess

An 18th-century British cartoon shows Catherine as entirely willing to make a pact with the Devil should such a contract guarantee her dominion over Poland (symbolized by its capital, Warsaw) and Turkey (symbolized by its capital, Constantinople).

CONSTANTINOPLE

WARSAW

QUEEN CATHERINES DREAM.

named Louise, who changed her religion, was baptized Elizabeth Alekseyevna, and became grand duchess. Catherine tried to persuade Alexander to replace his father as her successor, but he refused, claiming that he wanted only to live in peace. The empress gained no more satisfaction from her relationship with Paul, whose hatred for his mother and indifference to public opinion remained undiminished. He dressed his soldiers in Prussian uniforms and marched them up and down the grounds of his palace, just as Peter III had done. And, like Peter, he became increasingly unpopular and was suspected of madness. "The grand duke's head," said one high-ranking observer, "is filled with phantoms."

How can shoemakers meddle in affairs of state? A shoemaker only knows how to make shoes.
—CATHERINE THE GREAT
on the French Revolution

GIRAUDON/ART RESOURCE

In 1796 Catherine was 67 years old and her health was beginning to fail. But she was still an effective ruler. At the suggestion of her lover, Zubov, she engaged her oldest granddaughter, the 13-year-old Alexandra, to the new king of Sweden, Gustavus

Soldiers of the Republic of France stand guard at the execution of their former monarch, King Louis XVI (1754–1793). Louis's death, and the revolution that preceded it, greatly disturbed Catherine, who believed that the liberal, egalitarian ideas of French thinkers like Rousseau and Voltaire, her intellectual idols, had been responsible for the bloodshed.

Polish soldier and patriot General Thaddeus Kosciuszko (1746–1817), who initiated and led a rebellion against the Russian forces occupying his country in 1794. Following the suppression of the revolt, Kosciuszko, who had fought on the American side in the War of Independence, spent two years in prison in Russia.

IV, who was 18. Although the young couple fell in love the first time they met, disaster was to befall the intended match. When he arranged the details of the marriage, Zubov had failed to make it clear that Alexandra would not convert from the Russian Orthodoxy to Swedish Lutheranism. On September 2, 1796, the day of the betrothal ceremony, Gustavus was about to sign the marriage contract when he saw the clause specifying this. He refused to sign, and hours passed as the court waited. Finally, Zubov told Catherine what had happened. Grim-faced but calm, she announced that the young king was ill and that the ceremony would be postponed. Everyone knew that it was postponed forever. Alexandra fainted and Catherine retired to her private rooms. During the night, Catherine had a dizzy spell that was probably caused by a mild stroke. It was the beginning of the end for the empress and the beginning of a crisis over the succession.

Alexander had by this time become convinced that his father was completely mad. So shaken was he by his visits to Paul that he finally agreed to succeed his grandmother, who was now seriously ill. There were open sores on her legs and she was suffering from increasing stomach pain. Deciding not to wait, she wrote the manifesto changing the order of succession, planning to make the news public on her name day, November 24, 1796.

On the morning of November 5, Catherine awoke early and chatted pleasantly with her lady-in-waiting. Saying she had slept very well, the empress rubbed her face with ice and drank her usual strong, black coffee. She began working energetically on government papers with her secretaries and Zubov. Then she dismissed everyone and went into her bathroom. After some time had passed, her servants became uneasy. Hesitantly, they opened the door to Catherine's bathroom and found that she had collapsed. The empress was carried to her bed, still breathing but only with great difficulty. The doctors announced that they could do nothing, and the priests were sent for. When Paul heard that his mother was near death, he rushed to her bedside.

Following Catherine's death in 1796 at the age of 67, her son Paul, now Tsar Paul I, believing that Catherine had ordered the murder of his father, Peter III, had Peter's coffin placed alongside Catherine's, beneath a banner proclaiming "DIVIDED IN LIFE, JOINED IN DEATH."

Seeing that Catherine was dying, Paul ordered that all of his mother's personal papers be sorted—and burned. Among the documents consigned to the flames was the manifesto giving the throne to Alexander. On the night of November 6, 1796, at 10:15 P.M., Catherine drew her last breath. Within 24 hours, the palace was filled with the Prussian uniforms of Paul's troops. Catherine's detested son became Tsar Paul I.

Less than five years later, in 1801, Paul was assassinated. Among his murderers was Plato Zubov. Alexander then took the throne of Russia just as his grandmother had wished—the will of Catherine the Great had been triumphant once more.

Catherine, born a German, died a true Russian. Her 34-year reign brought both great advances and great misery to her adoptive people. Her main interests were cultural and political. Determined to make the backward Russian society as cultured as those of Germany and France, she introduced and encouraged literature, art, science, and new philosophical ideas to her adoptive people. She was the first Russian ruler to spend large sums of money on education. She founded new universities and the nation's first school for girls.

Catherine, who was herself a dedicated reader and art collector, encouraged both reading and appreciation of the arts among her nobles. She worked tirelessly to modernize and improve the structure of Russia's government. Although she thought of herself as a "republican," Catherine actually made Russia's already powerful ruling class even stronger, and she increased its power over the serfs. She began her reign feeling sympathy for the impoverished and mistreated peasants, but while she was empress, the number of people enslaved by cruel and greedy masters increased vastly. The serfs did not benefit from Catherine's fascination with founding new schools, encouraging new art, and promoting the philosophical ideals of the Enlightenment. In foreign affairs too, Catherine was extremely successful. During her reign, Russia greatly expanded its borders and increased its international prestige.

Catherine acquired her title of The Great largely in terms of her accomplishments in foreign affairs. She was operating within the value system of her century, which judged the achievement of monarchs largely in terms of the expansion of their frontiers and the magnitude of their military victories.

—L. JAY OLIVA

Catherine had many lovers, but she never allowed any of them to rule Russia. In part because she was a woman, her behavior was frequently criticized. Catherine's enemies could not, however, destroy the record of her accomplishments. She remains one of the most brilliant and influential sovereigns the world has ever known.

Ten years before she died, Catherine, perhaps partly in jest, wrote her own epitaph. The words were never actually inscribed on her tomb, but they leave a clear picture of the empress's view of herself:

"Here lies Catherine the Second, born in Stettin on April 21, 1729.

"In the year 1744 she went to Russia to marry Peter III. At the age of 14, she made the threefold resolution to please her husband, Elizabeth, and the nation. She neglected nothing to accomplish this.

> *Catherine's reign was therefore to see the completion of the orientation in favor of the nobility begun under Peter the Great's successors: their monopoly of key positions in the administration, the extension of their serf rights and their exemption from military obligations.*
> —LEO GERSHOY
> American historian

Tsar Alexander I, considered by many to have inherited his grandmother's political acumen, continued many of the liberal reforms that Catherine had instituted. He improved his country's educational system and introduced constitutional government to Finland and Poland, two of Russia's most important satellite states.

"Eighteen years of boredom and loneliness caused her to read many books.

"Having ascended the throne of Russia, she wished to do good and sought to procure for her subjects happiness, liberty, and prosperity.

"She pardoned readily and hated no one. Indulgent, easy to live with, possessed of a cheerful nature, a republican soul, and a kind heart, she had friends.

"Work was easy for her; she enjoyed society and the arts."

Dominating a square in Leningrad (formerly Petrograd, formerly St. Petersburg), a massive statue of Catherine stands at the heart of the city where she spent much of her time as grand duchess and as empress.

Further Reading

Dukes, P. *Catherine the Great and the Russian Nobility.* New York: Cambridge University Press, 1968.

Grey, Ian. *Catherine the Great: Autocrat and Empress of All Russia.* Westport, Connecticut: Greenwood Press, 1975.

Kochan, Miriam. *Catherine the Great.* New York: St. Martin's Press, Inc., 1977.

Oliva, L. Jay. *Catherine the Great.* Englewood Cliffs, New Jersey: Prentice-Hall, Inc., 1971.

Troyat, Henri. *Catherine the Great,* tr. Joan Pinkham. New York: Berkley Publishing Corp., 1981.

Chronology

April 21, 1729	Born Sophia Augusta Frederica, daughter of Christian August, prince of Anhalt-Zerbst, and Johanna Elizabeth, princess of Holstein-Gottorp, in Stettin
1740	Accession of infant Tsar Ivan VI, under regency of his mother, Anna Leopoldovna
Dec. 6, 1741	Elizabeth, daughter of Peter the Great, ousts Ivan VI and accedes to the throne of Russia
Feb. 20, 1744	Sophia and her mother arrive in Moscow at invitation of Empress Elizabeth
June 28, 1744	Converts to Russian Orthodox faith
June 29, 1744	Becomes officially engaged to Grand Duke Peter and takes name Catherine Alekseyevna
Aug. 21, 1745	Marries Grand Duke Peter in St. Petersburg
Sept. 20, 1754	Gives birth to son, Paul Petrovich, the future Tsar Paul I
1755	Begins affair with Polish nobleman Count Stanislaw Poniatowski
Dec. 25, 1761	Empress Elizabeth dies and is succeeded by her nephew, Tsar Peter III
June 28, 1762	Catherine, having overthrown Peter with help of supporters, is proclaimed empress of Russia
July 6, 1762	Peter strangled by Catherine's men while under house arrest
Sept. 22, 1762	Catherine crowned in Moscow
July 4, 1764	Former Tsar Ivan VI assassinated
1764–66	Catherine writes *Nakaz*, a treatise intended to serve as basis for new Russian legal code
Oct. 1768	Russian troops in pursuit of rebellious Cossacks violate Turkish border, inadvertently starting Catherine's first war with Turks
1773	French writer Denis Diderot visits Russia
1773	Russian army deserter Yemelyan Pugachov leads Cossacks and thousands of peasants in campaign against landlords
July 21, 1774	Peace of Kutchuk Kainardji signed, ending war with Turks
1774	Catherine initiates love affair with Potemkin
1774	Peasant revolt suppressed and Pugachov executed
July 23, 1783	Russia officially annexes the Crimea
1785–92	Russia at war again with Turks
1788–90	Russia at war with Sweden
1795	Russia takes control of much of Poland
Nov. 6, 1796	Catherine dies, aged 67, in St. Petersburg, and is succeeded by Paul I

Index

Leslie McGuire, a graduate of Barnard College, was a contributing editor to the *Concise Columbia Encyclopedia*, and has written many books for children. She is also the author of *Napoleon* in the Chelsea House series WORLD LEADERS PAST & PRESENT.

Arthur M. Schlesinger, jr., taught history at Harvard for many years and is currently Albert Schweitzer Professor of the Humanities at City University of New York. He is the author of numerous highly praised works in American history and has twice been awarded the Pulitzer Prize. He served in the White House as special assistant to presidents Kennedy and Johnson.